PRAISE FOR *MOVE PAST YOUR PAIN: DISCOVER YOUR PURPOSE*

"Move Past Your Pain" is a masterful expression of hope and help from someone who has assisted thousands of people to come into a place of freedom and flourishing. Dr. Simms shares powerful personal stories and real-time accounts of others who have overcome life's shadow side. These examples will become a springboard for you to discover how to get free from past pain and move toward wholeness and healthy relationships. *—John Hansen, Lead Pastor Centerpoint Church, Murrieta, Ca.*

Through her background of growing up in a difficult environment, Mary has been given insight, passion, and compassion for her clients. Through this book, Mary hopes to pass this knowledge on to others so they too may discover a life of purpose, meaning, and contentment. *— Susan Titus Osborn, Author of over 30 books and Director of Christian Communicator Manuscript Critique Service*

Dr. Simms captures the essence of life-transforming principles. Practical wisdom is united with the fire of faith and leaves the reader with the understanding of how to change and the hope to do so. This book should be required reading for anyone who is tired of being held back from a higher level of living. *—Rev. Dr. Larry Walkemeyer, Lead Pastor, Light and Life Christian Fellowship North, Long Beach, Ca. Central Superintendent FMCSC, Coauthor of* 15 Characteristics of Effective Pastors

[Dr. Mary's] work offers tools for reversing negative generational patterns that will result in creating positive, purposeful legacies that will bring belonging and significance. —*Wil and Jacquie Chevalier, Executive Directors and Cofounders of LifeBranch Institute International, and authors of over fifteen books*

It is a privilege to endorse your book, *Move Past Your Pain: Discover Your Purpose.* It is engrossing and informative. The diverse case examples you give help readers learn how to apply the principles you teach to a wide variety of life situations. Your use of your personal journey is very moving and adds authenticity to the premise of the book. Readers will greatly benefit from reading this very fine book. —Dr. *Helen A. Mendes Love, MSW, Author of* God's Stress Management Plan *and* Reflections on the Upsides of Aging, Living with Joy and Purpose After Age 50

In this book, Dr. Simms uses powerful tools to prove the ancient truth: through the power of stories and the power of personal experience with Jesus Christ, God can redeem you from any place life has you. —*Charles Latchison, Lead Pastor, Light and Life Christian Fellowship West, Long Beach, Ca.*

Move Past Your Pain: Discover Your Purpose

Overcoming Negative Generational Patterns to Achieve Your Best Life

DR. MARY M. SIMMS

WestBow
PRESS®
A DIVISION OF THOMAS NELSON
& ZONDERVAN

WestBow Press books may be ordered through booksellers or by contacting:

WestBow Press
A Division of Thomas Nelson & Zondervan
1663 Liberty Drive
Bloomington, IN 47403
www.westbowpress.com
1 (866) 928-1240

Credit for images: Azenith Gueco

ISBN: 978-1-5127-3188-0 (sc)
ISBN: 978-1-5127-3187-3 (e)

Library of Congress Control Number: 2016902720

Print information available on the last page.

WestBow Press rev. date: 3/11/2016

DEDICATION

To my mom, Mary Mitchell, who has gone
on but has taught me to love God
and live with integrity, hope, and purpose.

"I have come that you might have life … abundantly."

Jesus of Nazareth

CONTENTS

LIST OF FIGURES

ACKNOWLEDGMENTS

With gratitude to:

My husband of over forty years, Martin, who is always there for me, willing to serve and help.

Wil and Jacquie Chevalier, founders of LifeBranch Institute International and great role models both in writing and in serving others.

Jeff and Lynn Carr, who are great friends and encouraged me to write to help others.

INTRODUCTION

*I know what I am doing. I have it all planned
out—plans to take care of you, not abandon you,
plans to give you the future you hope for.*
—JEREMIAH 29:11 (MSG)

Do you know that you were created for purpose and meaning? It's true! There is a God-given purpose designed for each person. Regardless of a person's background or economic status, every life is significant.

Are you walking in your purpose? Do you wake up every day feeling passionate about your purpose? Walking in your purpose is about using your God-given gifts and talents to bring personal satisfaction and fulfillment, and then using those gifts to influence other lives.

Are you living your best life? Living your best life is about pursuing a purposeful and productive life, thereby modeling and establishing a positive legacy for the next generation.

Like so many others, you may have a desire to live your best life, but may find yourself stuck because of well-worn negative patterns that continue to plague you and prevent you from achieving your goals and dreams.

If this describes your current situation, then this book is for you. Having ministered to thousands of people as a family therapist and minister for almost three decades, I have seen how negative generational cycles are repeated, causing major psychological damage and unhappiness, not only for individuals, but for their families also. Our past patterns, both positive and negative, can affect the choices that we make for our future. It is important to understand the patterns of our past and how they shape us, so that we can make changes and choices that will bring health, abundant life, and purpose for our future!

These negative generational patterns emerge from behaviors that we saw modeled while growing up and are now manifested in our life. These patterns can include poor self-image, rejection, anger, substance abuse (either drugs or alcohol), sex addictions, sex abuse, adultery, dishonesty, emotional and physical abuse, unhealthy lifestyle choices, poor money management, poor conflict management, inability to handle anger, negative and destructive thinking, economic instability, and unforgiveness. Also included are patterns of deception, living in denial, avoidance, lying, running away, not facing issues, fear of relationships, and finally, settling for less than God's best.

This book will help you identify the negative patterns that have impacted your life and kept you from moving forward and maximizing your God-given purpose. Once these patterns are identified, you have the responsibility to adopt new patterns that lead to living a free and fully functional life.

This book provides tools for reversing negative generational patterns, resulting in the creation of both positive and purposeful legacies to bring belonging and significance to people everywhere. You have the power, with God's great help in your work of recovery, to live the life you desire. In *Move Past Your Pain: Discover Your Purpose*, you will learn that you can implement positive change. My prayer is that this book will assist you in identifying the negative generational patterns that have hindered you and made your life difficult.

God loves you and has a purpose and plan for your life, no matter where you came from or what has happened in your past. He is in the restoration and transformation business! His love for you is unconditional, pure, and simple. It is not based on your performance or in what family system you grew up. Because of Christ's finished work on the cross, there is hope for eliminating the negative generational patterns and emotional pain that hinder your purpose and keep you from living a fulfilled life.

Many of the examples in this book are modeled after actual cases, nevertheless, the names and details have been changed to protect confidentiality.

CHAPTER 1

My Story

*To bestow on them a crown of beauty instead of
ashes, the oil of gladness instead of mourning, and a
garment of praise instead of a spirit of despair.*
—ISAIAH 61:3 (NIV)

My personal story is an example of how God used brokenness and suffering to reshape a life to achieve His great purpose. Growing up in one of the roughest areas of New York City, Bedford Stuyvesant in Brooklyn, I heard firsthand the sounds of violence, hopelessness, and despair at an early age. We lived in daily fear of the violent crime spawned, at least in part, by the poverty that was all around us. Drug dealing and using, gang violence, domestic violence, burglaries, rapes, and all sorts of violent and petty crimes were part of everyday life in our neighborhood. Our streets were full of the kind of urban ills that keep people chained to a life of poverty, violence, and abuse.

I was only eight, and my sister, Jacquie, was nine when I awakened one night from a sound sleep. "What is that noise that sounded like a big bang?" I asked her. We hid under our beds as gunshots thundered through our living room, just a few feet from where we lay.

"Don't go out there! Stay in here," my sister screamed. My heart pounded in fear as the bullets pierced our living room walls, shattering the windows and increasing our terror. Unfortunately, this had become an all-too-familiar scene. When we left for school the next morning, we saw the telltale signs of violence left by the blood that had spilled on the sidewalk the night before.

On another occasion, I remember walking home from school with Jacquie and Mom, and as we started to enter the apartment, we heard the dog barking loudly. My sister screamed, "Don't go in the house! The door has been forced open!"

Terrified, I ran upstairs to the second floor where my aunt and uncle lived. My mom and sister stayed to talk to the police. When my sister said, "You can come home now, Mary," I pretended that I did not hear her, because I did not want to go home. I did not feel safe there. Later, I learned that the blood splattered throughout our house came from the bites our large German shepherd had taken out of the burglar as he tried to find a way out. That was just one of the many times our house was robbed in the middle of the day.

My dad was stabbed on two occasions, and fighting often broke out in the neighborhood. Living with fear and anxiety was what I knew as a child. I was always afraid that my dad might be hurt or killed and would not come home. Back then, our neighborhood was one of the hardest, roughest, and most unforgiving areas of New York City. Most people who left did so by way of death, drugs, or detention. Although both my mom and dad had strong work ethics, more often than not, Mom carried the family both emotionally and financially. My dad was an alcoholic, and when he drank, he always projected blame and anger on my mom.

I remember when my mom took dad to see the movie *The Days of Wine and Roses*. The hope was that it would wake him up about his denial related to his drinking. Instead, he continued to project blame and stay in denial. As soon as the movie was over, Dad said, "That lady in that movie reminded me of you, always nagging that poor man."

I remember another incident when Dad started drinking and became more and more critical. He would pick on any little thing to start an argument and to project blame onto my mother. "Don't nag me about the time that I come home. I can come home anytime I dang well please!" he proclaimed. "You are making me angry."

Mom responded, "Jack, I just thought you were hurt or something. I was concerned." The tension escalated to the point of destructive anger. At that point, he pinned Mom in a corner.

"Daddy, Daddy," I screamed, "please don't hurt Mommy!" I jumped in between them, trying to protect my mom.

"Stop!" my sister yelled. She did her best to keep me out of harm's way.

Dad had a proud heritage as an African-American military man. He was part of the 761st Tank Battalion, the legendary all-black tank unit that became famous for their heroic efforts during World War II. Mom said that when he came home from the war, he was just not the same.

As a soldier, he had experienced all kinds of horrific violence. Dad witnessed one of his nineteen-year-old best friends decapitated with a sword during a battle. It wasn't until many years later, when I became a clinician, that I realized my father had suffered from post-traumatic stress disorder and turned to alcohol as a way of coping. And, like many who use alcohol or other substances to ease their pain, he became physically abusive to my mom when he drank. But he never acknowledged or admitted that he needed help. Although we loved our dad, my sister and I, even though only twelve and eleven, began to encourage our mother to leave the toxic environment behind. My mom was a very merciful person and wanted to get help for my dad, but he was a person who did not believe that he needed help.

My mom had a strong relationship with a living and loving God, and we always saw her praying for direction and for God to help her to make life-changing decisions. One day, she announced to my sister and me that we were going to visit her sister Billie who was sick with breast cancer. Billie lived in Louisiana. Mom's other sister, Lucille, lived in Arizona and knew of our situation. She invited us to come and stay there to live.

Mom decided to go to Louisiana in spite of Dad's threats of what he would do to her if we left.

"Girls, we're leaving. We are going to visit my sister who is ill," she quietly told us one day. Both my sister and I did not have to be convinced. We were beyond ready and willing!

Two nights before we went to the train station, some of our belongings sat packed into one large suitcase. We hid the suitcase under blankets so that Dad would not find it. We were fearful that if he discovered that we were leaving, he would physically hurt our mother. Dad walked into the room and saw the blankets that were covering the suitcases, but he just looked and moved on. It was as if something blinded his eyes so that he could not see what we were up to. My sister and I were shocked and relieved that he did not ask about the suitcase, and we were more relieved when we got on that train two days later.

So, we decided to leave our painful times behind and move to a safer, more peaceful place. I was twelve and my sister was thirteen and a half when we made our escape.

We left New York with very few resources. All Mom had was an active prayer life and a determination to seek something better. She cashed in her life insurance policies and hid our meager belongings in a locker at Penn Station until the day we took the train to Louisiana.

Although Mom contemplated returning to Brooklyn after helping her sister in Louisiana, Aunt Lucille in Tucson convinced Mom that going back to Brooklyn would be a bad decision for all of us. "Mary (my mother's name was Mary also), that environment is not a good one for raising those girls. If you want to remain healthy and provide safety for your children, you need to get them away from there. You and the girls can live here with us until you land on your feet."

So, with the support of my aunt and her family, we moved to Tucson. When we settled in, Mom went back to school and obtained her nursing credentials so that she could support us as a single parent. Our lives changed drastically after that. Mom got a good job, and my sister and I attended college.

After getting married and starting my own family, my husband encouraged me to continue my educational process. He could see the "calling" on my life and wanted me to be fully equipped for the task of empowering people in their recovery and in their journey. I went on to obtain two master's degrees and a Ph.D. Watching Mom's level of integrity and tenacity sparked a burning desire and passion inside of me. That passion was the thing that drove me to prepare myself for the work that I was called to do—inspiring purpose and passion into the lives of others. After getting my education and training, I founded a clinic designed to help people find emotional health so they could possess all that God has for them. I believe He called me to influence others so that lives can be restored and positive, purposeful legacies created and established.

Shortly after that, and only in his forties, Dad had a stroke due to his alcoholism. He stayed in a rehabilitation institution for seven years. There, he stayed sober for a long time, and we started communicating by phone. In the rehab institution, he made beautiful leather purses for my sister and me, which he mailed to us. That was a time of healing and comfort for me as I felt valued and cared for by my dad, even though it was a long-distance relationship. Unfortunately, when he was released from rehab, he went back to the same environment and set of friends that he previously had, and the drinking started again.

After leaving New York at the age of eleven, I never saw my dad alive again. I received a message from my uncle that my dad had passed shortly before his fifty-fourth birthday. I was twenty-one years old. I had a lot of grieving and loss to process. I needed to work through all of the lost years of not having him around. Every time I flew into New York to visit relatives, I visited the Veterans cemetery where dad was buried. On one particular occasion, my husband drove me to the cemetery and I began to think about my dad. The tears welled up. Then in the quiet, peaceful, beautifully green environment of the cemetery, I felt the urge of uncontrollable grief. As the tears started to flow hard, I began to cry out to God to understand what the grieving was about. After all, it had been many years since Dad had been gone. Why was this uncontrollable sobbing hitting me at this moment? I began to understand that the grief represented all of the years that I missed out on a relationship with my dad because of his love relationship with alcohol. I thought about the brilliant man that he once was, and that he would never know my children or be able to impact their lives because of his choices and disease. Besides having an excellent technical acumen, he was also a great photographer. I thought about all of the abilities he had and how he did not fully use his God given-gifts because his life was cut short due to his drinking. Then, all of a sudden, some lessons came for me. I saw that as an adult with options and choices, I could learn from Dad's life. Jesus also reminded me that although it was sad that Dad missed opportunities and blessings in his life due to his drinking, I had a choice to do something different in my life. I was empowered as a young adult, then in my early thirties, to make sure that I never adopted a pattern of allowing any substance or thing to control my life and my thinking. I had the option to make different choices than he did. I went to the cemetery feeling sad and hopeless, and left feeling empowered and hopeful! What I felt God communicate to me was that my dad made choices that affected his life in negative ways. Yet, because I knew Christ and recognized His sovereignty over my life, I could make choices that would influence my life in positive ways and build a wonderful legacy for my children. The exciting news was I could reverse this generational pattern with God's help!

CHAPTER 2

Patterns That Repeat

*I decide to do good, but I don't really do it; I decide not
to do bad, but then I do it anyway. My decisions, such as
they are, don't result in actions. Something has gone wrong
deep within me and gets the better of me every time.*
—ROMANS 7:19-20 (MSG)

Growing up, I had a wonderful mother, and she always taught us to work hard and treat people with kindness and respect. However, there were some things about my mom that I took issue with, such as asking too many questions at what I thought was the wrong time. One day I was so frustrated with my mom for "prying" into my business that I jokingly told both my son and daughter that if I ever acted like my mom in that way, they should just "shoot me." One day I was engaging in the same behavior as my mom. Both my kids laughed and said, "Mom, where is the gun?" I include this illustration to show that we do not always see our blind spots and the repeated patterns or behaviors that we dislike in ourselves. I think we have to be willing to have a sense of humor and a willingness to ask God to give us an accurate picture of ourselves.

In working with so many over the years, I have seen how the desire not to repeat a negative pattern is there, but sometimes it still happens. Some of the statements that I've heard from people with whom I've worked over the years talk about how they did not mean to repeat the pattern that they grew up with, but they find themselves in a situation doing just the opposite of their desired outcome.

"I will never make the choices that my dad made," James said. Yet, at forty years old, he found himself drinking to cope with a difficult marriage and financial hardship.

"I never thought that I would be in a similar situation as my mom at forty-six years old," Susan reported. "I vowed that I would only marry once, and here I am, just like my mom, working on my third marriage."

"I know how it feels to be neglected as a child, and here I am doing the same thing to my children, looking for love in all of the wrong places," Diane confessed, pain etched across her face.

"Dad's drug of choice was alcohol," Evan shared. "Although I did not repeat his pattern, I use marijuana every day. I vowed that I would never use anything that would impair my judgment and cause me not to focus. Now I find myself feeling trapped and powerless, and I don't know what to do about it."

Nane heaved out a big sigh. "My mom could never keep a job, and I decided that would never happen to me. Yet, I have been fired from five jobs in the last ten years."

Genograms and Patterns

It is difficult to change what we don't know about.

On a recent trip to Yellowstone National Park, the ranger gave us written information warning us to stay at least 100 yards away from the bison. In that bison roam so freely and look so docile, some people think that it is not a big deal to get five or six feet away from them to get that prize-winning, close-up photo. The reality is that there have been injuries from bison goring people because they got too close. This example illustrates how becoming aware of the facts in a situation enlightens you as to what you need to do to stay safe. Awareness is a powerful principle.

One tool that helps people become aware of the patterns in their lives and how to live safely and well is the use of genograms.

I make a practice of doing a genogram for every person who comes into my office. Genograms are a way of visually looking at family patterns and history over the past two or three generations. Most of my clients really enjoy this assignment, and they learn valuable lessons from them. Genograms are like maps. A map is a drawing that helps us find the location of where we want to go. Genograms are similar to maps in that they help us to see where we would like to go in our future. If we can look at the past patterns in our family history, we can embrace the patterns that have been positive and healthy and that have contributed to producing good fruit in our lives. We can also be alert to our negative patterns and learn what not to repeat.

An example is a picture of the parents, grandparents, and great-grandparents who all went through divorce. The key is in understanding what the patterns are so that we can learn both from the positive and negative sides of our history. Once awareness comes, we now have an opportunity with God's great help to do something about it.

Pattern of Generational Alcoholism

Below is a case story about how alcoholism affected a family for the past three generations.

Margo had four brothers and three sisters. She was next-to-the-youngest. Her dad was an alcoholic and her mom only drank socially.

"My dad had a great job. He just drank on the weekends," Margo said.

"How much did he drink?" I asked.

"I don't really know, but he was always on the couch passed out every Saturday and Sunday night."

Margo described her dad as a functional alcoholic, as he worked a lot and did his binge drinking on the weekends. Margo found alcohol in her dad's closet when she was ten years old. As a teenager, she and her friends would sneak around and drink. Fortunately for her, she hated the taste and vowed that she would never drink. However, three of her four brothers are either alcoholics or moving in that direction. The younger brother is a drug user. As you can see from the genogram in Figure 1 entitled "Generational Patterns that Repeat," the substance abuse/alcoholism pattern repeated in three generations starting with Margo's grandfather on her dad's side. Her dad was also an alcoholic and, as you can see in this case, all of the male children became alcoholics or drug dependent. In our work together, the genogram opened Margo's eyes to how much she had been affected by growing up in an alcoholic family system. Margo came to realize that she attracted men who were emotionally unavailable, just like her dad had been.

She also felt that she had a difficult time managing conflict in relationships. In her life growing up, issues were never dealt with until a crisis occurred. Margo had a lot of emotional and financial stress in her life, as she had established a pattern of waiting until things got out of control before she did something about it.

Once Margo became aware of the negative patterns she was living with, she could start establishing and implementing behaviors in her life that would assist in stopping the pattern. Although difficult, she began to make a practice and discipline of learning how to face things that were hard to deal with instead of pretending that a problem would go away by itself. As she learned to develop the new habits and the discipline not to return to the same old coping pattern that she was comfortable with (although miserable), her life started to feel more in control.

It takes work, courage, and prayer to look at these patterns, because doing so can be emotionally painful. However, once you are able to look back at the pattern with the eyes of an adult instead of a child, you can then be empowered with God's great help to make the changes that will ultimately lead to your best life!

Listed below are some principles for thoughtful reflection that summarize the chapter:

1. Be aware of both the positive and negative patterns from your past and how they have affected your relationships, marriage, identity, etc., in the present.

2. Invite God into your situation to open your eyes to negative behaviors that may contribute to keeping you stuck.

3. Understand that, as a child, you did not have the power or control to change anything; however, as an adult, you are not powerless; you are empowered with cognitive ability and resources to change your circumstances.

4. Develop an action plan that will assist you in unhooking from negative patterns and help you adopt new ways that will lead to healthy lifestyle choices.

Figure 1: Generational Patterns that can Repeat without Intervention

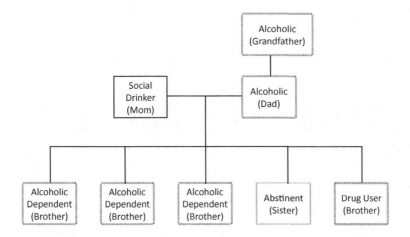

CHAPTER 3

Stress and Patterns

Are you tired? Worn out? Burned out on religion? Come to me. Get away with me and you'll recover your life. I'll show you how to take a real rest. Walk with me and work with me—watch how I do it. Learn the unforced rhythms of grace. I won't lay anything heavy or ill-fitting on you. Keep company with me and you'll learn to live freely and lightly.
—MATTHEW 11:28-30 (MSG)

A simple dictionary definition of *stress* from *Merriam-Webster* is: a state of mental tension and worry caused by problems in your life, work, etc. If you live any length of time, you know that life can be stressful. In fact, Jesus said in His Word that trouble will come, but that He is the one we can depend on in getting through the trials of life. "I have told you these things, so that in me you may have peace. In this world you will have trouble. But take heart! I have overcome the world" (John 16:33 NIV). Even though we know as believers that we can trust in and rely on God to help us move through the challenges we face, sometimes life's burdens and circumstances can get so heavy that we feel overwhelmed, hopeless, and powerless.

Not all stress is bad, according to Dr. Helen Mendes, author of *God's Stress Management Plan, Ten Biblical Principles for Avoiding, Reducing or Better Managing Stress.* She writes, "Some degree of stress is necessary for our growth, health, and safety. As an adult, the concerns you feel about the potential threats to your life and health motivates you to avoid driving your car at 110 miles an hour, especially, along a darkened, unfamiliar road. It is when we experience too much of it for too long a time, that stress can harm us." She goes on to say, "We can trigger our mind-body alarm system whenever we obsess about the bad things that can happen to us or our loved ones. If our stress responses are frequently triggered or go on for long periods of time, we can become ill. The longer the time that level of stress lasts, the more potential harm it can do to you. Stress that goes on for a long time is called Chronic Stress."

A Chronic Stress Story

Meet Jane. She grew up in a home where her mom was chronically stressed and depressed. When financial or relationship difficulties came into her mother's life, she just literally went to sleep. Her mom did not know how to handle the trouble in her marriage or in her finances, so she just ignored the problems and pretended that they would go away. She felt overwhelmed, powerless, and slept a lot. As a result, Jane had to step up to take care of her sisters and brothers, since she was the oldest. Fast forward to the present. Jane is forty-two and having similar issues in her life. She is finding herself wanting to handle the problems in her life the same way her mom did. She feels stuck because she works long hours, and it isn't practical for her to sleep her life away—she has to pay her bills! However, the anxiety is now overwhelming because of the stress she feels, so she is on several anti-depressant medications to put a Band-Aid on the problems. Certainly, the medication is helping to raise the serotonin levels in her brain so that her mood is not so blue. She finds herself able to function at work while on the meds, but still feels overwhelmed and powerless, the same feelings that she had when she was a little girl. As she comes into counseling, she discovers that the pattern of holding negative emotions inside and just continuing to stir them around without taking action was part of the pattern in which she grew up. As a child, she did not have the choice or the voice to change anything. However, as an adult, she could begin to see that she had the option to take action steps to make changes.

Change is difficult because it requires coming out of a comfort zone that continues to be well worn, comfortable, and familiar. It takes knowledge, understanding, and faith to change ingrained negative patterns. In addition to dealing with the difficulty of changing a well-worn pattern, negative emotions such as fear and worry can also get in the way of positive movement. Anger can keep us stuck. So much energy is focused on the negative that there is not much room left in our thinking to focus on what is good about our situation. Anger has a way of creating its own level of stress in that it keeps us stuck in feelings of bitterness and resentment, which can lead to destructive consequences.

Anger Patterns Resulting From Abuse

Mona is an example of someone who had repeated stress in her life due to a pattern of anger, which had its roots in having been molested by a relative when she was a young girl of seven years. She was continually threatened by the molester, who used intimidation and fear to convince her not to tell anyone. The abuse went on for four years until she moved away and did not see the person again. She is now forty years old and has never married. In her early adult life, she had several relationships, but each time the relationship started to become serious, Mona would make an excuse for why it just would not work out and always found a reason to get angry so that she could end the relationship. After several of these failed attempts, she decided to come into counseling. Mona also reported that she was starting to develop stomach problems, and her primary care doctor suggested that she get into counseling to find out what was going on. After a few sessions, it became clear to me that she had a lot of unresolved anger toward the molester, but she often directed the anger at the current person she was in relationship with.

"Did you ever confront your abuser?" I asked.

"No, we just moved on like nothing happened. My mom did not find out about it until I grew up and moved out of the house."

"How did she find out?"

"I knew I had to tell her because she kept blaming me for not being able to keep a relationship. In my heart, I secretly blamed her for what happened."

"Why did you blame her—did you feel she did not protect you?"

"Looking back, I know she had to work a lot being a single parent, and this was a relative that she trusted and respected. Yet, I still blamed her for what happened. Once my mom and I got into a huge argument, and not only did the secret of my molestation come out, but also I blurted out to her, 'You are the cause of me not being able to get married because you allowed this to come into my life!' I think I just stuffed all of my anger and blamed it on my mom and then transferred those angry feelings to the men in my life."

After working with Mona for several months and helping her look at the deep anger and resentment she carried, she was able to see the connection between what happened to her as a powerless little girl and the trauma that she experienced through adult eyes. She was so used to harboring the deeply buried anger and resentment that it had become a way of life for her. Any reasonable person would say that Mona had a right to be angry about what happened to her; however, the anger that she continued to feel when she got into a new relationship was keeping her from enjoying healthy intimacy.

As Mona began to see how her anger was affecting her life and relationships, she began to see the need to heal from the anger that she had been carrying. She could see how she used the anger as a way of protecting herself from further hurt. She was also able to see how she was staying stuck in her anger, which was preventing her from moving forward to achieve her goal of getting into a healthy, intimate, lifelong relationship.

A tool in learning how to manage the stress is to identify the root cause of it. For Mona, she harbored intense anger, and she was so used to living with this anger that it had become a way of life for her. She was not aware of how it was affecting her physical body until her doctor mentioned that her stomach problem could be related to some sort of stress in her life. Emotionally, she had put up walls so that people could not get close to her. This affected her ability to trust safe people and have healthy relationships.

Boundaries and Stress

Often, circumstances out of our control can add to a lot of stress in our lives. A loved one gets sick suddenly. A friend incurs a traumatic brain injury caused by a car accident. A young child needs help and so does an elderly parent, both at the same time. However, there are other times when we make decisions out of our inability to set healthy boundaries, which contributes to our stress level. One of the very helpful tools in managing stress is the ability to set boundaries for the people with whom we live and work. Boundaries are a necessary part of living. They help keep our lives balanced so that we don't become overwhelmed by too much stress.

Picture a boundary as an emotional fence that needs to be lowered when we feel safe and available to others, and raised when we start juggling too many balls. Also, think of a boundary as a rain sensor. The sprinkler system works every day and is set to water the plants at a certain time. However, if it senses that it is raining outside, the system shuts down. There is no need for the automatic sprinkler if the rain is already doing the job.

If you are staying in your lane and handling the responsibilities assigned to you on a daily basis, there is no need to take on the responsibility to step in another person's lane. Think of a boundary as a necessary tool that helps us maintain a balanced and peaceful life. Boundaries are important because when used in healthy ways, they provide balance and can reduce our level of stress. The following account is a great example of someone who did not learn how to set up boundaries, and as a result, suffered a lot of unnecessary anxiety.

Dasa's story

Dasa, a thirty-one-year-old woman, came to see me because her medical doctor suggested that she get into counseling to find out why she was having such severe anxiety attacks. (Dasa had been rushed to a hospital because she thought that she was having a heart attack.) After taking Dasa's history, I found that her house had recently gone into foreclosure and she lost her job, all in the same year.

"Wow, that is a lot to go through all in one year. Do you have a good support system?" I asked.

"Well, not really. I've tried that before, and I've been taken advantage of before. So, I kind of stick to myself."

"Would you like to tell me about your experiences with the people who have hurt you?"

As Dasa shared, it became clear that she had both family members and friends who took advantage of her financially. "I really did not have the money to lend my cousin," she said. "But she needed to pay back a debt she owed, so I let her use my credit card. Now I'm in trouble because I don't have access to any more credit. My card is maxed out!"

Since she had a difficult time setting healthy boundaries, she coped by staying away from people and tried to deal with her issues all by herself. Having two major stressful events happening in one year, as well as Dasa carrying her burdens all by herself, were instrumental in her developing severe anxiety.

As Dasa learned that God created us for relationships and that she was not designed to carry the burdens all by herself, she began to develop the courage to establish safer, healthier relationships. Dasa had a positive faith in Christ, but she did not like His people. She did not go to church because she feared that people there would take advantage of her. She also had a tough time not viewing God as a punitive parent who delighted in punishing her. The authority figures in her life were not good stewards of her emotional and physical well-being.

Dasa started moving forward by connecting with a few people in a small, women's Bible study group at church. This class was non-threatening since it was not centered on her issues, but just a coming together to study God's Word. She felt safe and welcomed there. After attending the group for six weeks, she found another study at the same church. After a few months, she decided that she would attend the church services regularly.

As we worked on helping her figure out how to set healthy boundaries with both family members and friends, Dasa began to feel more confident that she could connect with others and develop healthy relationships.

Emotions and Stress

Past, unresolved emotional pain and misdirected anger often contribute to stressful patterns in our lives. If we are carrying around emotional baggage from the past, it may stay hidden until a situation occurs that can affect our current and future relationships.

Angel is an example of someone who was carrying around a lot of anger from his past, and it was affecting his relationship with his wife. Angel did not see that he was directing anger toward his wife that was actually intended for his mom. Let's look at his story.

Angel's Passive-Aggressive Pattern

Angel came from a family where his mom clearly wore the pants, and his dad was passive. Therefore, it was no surprise that when he fell in love and married, he chose a wife just like his mom. Soon after the honeymoon was over, he started having problems communicating with his wife, citing what he claimed were her controlling ways.

"My wife is so controlling that I can't even speak to her," Angel said, every time he came to see me. And while he had no problem saying these words to me, he seemed unable to express himself clearly to his wife.

Visit after visit, Angel rehearsed just how he would approach his wife when he went home and what he would say. However, once he was face-to-face with her, he couldn't bring himself to communicate his feelings. The excuse was always the same: "Well, it won't do any good. She never listens to me, and I feel as if I married my mother."

"Why do you say that?" I asked.

"Because she is so controlling. It is always her way or else!"

"Or else what?"

"I don't know. I always go along for fear of her wrath."

"Are you harboring resentment for just going along with your wife's ideas?"

"Of course, and she wonders why I like to spend a lot of time away from home."

"Perhaps you need to communicate and let her know how you are really feeling, instead of building up so much resentment inside."

Angel married a woman with control issues, just like his mom. However, this woman was not his mom, but his wife. Angel unconsciously repeated the pattern he learned in childhood. The more he internalized his anger and resentment, the more difficult it became for him to verbalize his true feelings. Angel could not see how his emotional brokenness and negative transference issues with his mom had wounded him, and how those wounds affected his relationship with his wife.

As Angel continued in counseling, he found the courage to start looking at himself instead of always blaming his spouse for the conflict. He then began to see that he had a lot of misdirected anger at his mom, and as an adult, he needed to face it instead of allowing it to come out when a conflict occurred with his wife. He had a problem taking ownership of his anger, which became very explosive sometimes. He felt it was better to stuff his feelings since they were so intense. He was afraid of his reactions. In counseling, Angel learned how to be honest with his anger and to understand the emotions produced by his anger. He learned how to use his voice in constructive ways. He also learned that his anger was attached to some unforgiveness issues toward his mom. The unforgiveness was getting in the way of cultivating real intimacy with his wife. As he began to work toward identifying some of the root causes of the anger with his mom, he was able to talk about it and look at it through adult eyes. He started seeing the need to actively forgive his mom and release the resentments toward her over to God. Instead of carrying around a heavy load of anger, Angel started feeling emotionally lighter. He also felt more freedom to communicate his needs and feelings more effectively to his wife. As a result, Angel is enjoying a much more satisfying relationship with his wife and with others.

Managing Negative Emotions

Working through anger that has its roots in the past requires real self-reflection and an understanding of how to manage and control emotions. Some believe that they are being displeasing to God when they show their anger. Yet, they may keep their anger in and then act it out in passive-aggressive ways. An example of this is the case of ignoring or punishing a person in unrelated ways instead of communicating true feelings and expressing how the situation has affected them. God tells us in Scripture that it is okay to be angry, but do not become destructive with it. Let's look at Ephesians 4:26 (NIV): "In your anger do not sin; Do not let the sun go down while you are still angry." In other words, learn to recover quickly and resolve conflict so that you are not holding on to negative emotions or grudges.

From the back of our home, we can see the sun setting each evening. When we first moved in, I was delighted and awed to watch the sunsets every night and to behold the amazing hues and picturesque landscape with the mountains in the background. As the days went by and I got used to seeing this picture daily, I started taking it for granted, no longer delighting in it, unless my husband or a guest reminded me of how beautiful it was. We often do the same thing with our loved ones. We tend to take people who are close to us for granted and allow anger, resentments, or negative emotions to get in the way.

As human beings, we have the capacity to experience myriad emotions. It is actually a wonderful gift to be able to feel emotions. Can you imagine a world in which people don't feel anything at all? It would not only be boring, but robotic. The key is to be able to manage our emotions so that we don't hurt ourselves or others. Our anger, if not guided by reason and conscience, can have destructive consequences. A good illustration of this principle is Maria.

Maria's story

Maria is attracted to Bill but is married to Steve. She is tempted to have an affair with Bill because she is struggling in her relationship with Steve. Maria's God-given conscience, plus her ability to reason, helps her realize that it would be destructive for everyone concerned to enter into an emotional and physical affair with Bill. If she engaged in this behavior, her marriage could be over and her children would feel betrayed. When she looks forward and thinks about the consequences of her potential actions, she decides that she does not want to repeat the pattern that her mom modeled—walking out on her family when Maria was only thirteen to pursue another man. Maria's reasoning ability helped her to remember the emotional pain that she had suffered when her mom left. Maria had then vowed that her future children would never suffer the feelings of abandonment, heartache, and emptiness that she had suffered by not having her mom around. The memory of the emotional pain also helped her to recall the weight of her mother's choices. In spite of her previous vow, Maria realized that she was now experiencing, as an adult, a strong pull toward a man whom she felt was giving her emotional support. In this situation, she could easily repeat her mom's pattern because of the emotional tugs on her heart. However, the emotional pain resulting from her mother's choices during Maria's childhood helped her realize that it would be devastating for her to repeat her mom's pattern, hurting her own children the way she had been hurt.

A great principle to employ is what I call RCO, **R**easoning the **C**onsequences all the way **O**ut, prior to making a decision. This principle helps you not to give in to the feelings you are experiencing in the moment of crisis, but instead consider the entire picture.

I stated earlier that our past emotional pain and hurts, as well as poor modeling, can often lead to more stress in our lives and cause us to experience less than God's best. Let's look at a few more case stories.

June's Commitment Problem

"So why don't you want to get married? You've been with John for over ten years," I asked June, a successful businesswoman with serious commitment issues. She was in an on-and-off relationship that went into the off mode every time her boyfriend mentioned marriage.

"Well, my mother was married to my dad, but he cheated on her throughout their marriage and she was just miserable. I'm not going to put myself in a situation where I can get hurt," June replied.

"Has John ever been unfaithful to you?" I asked.

"No," she replied, "or we wouldn't be together now."

"What makes you think taking your relationship to the next logical step will make him change the way he behaves with you? What about that word *commitment*? It seems he's the one who is committed to you, but are you able to reciprocate the same to him?"

"After all those years of seeing how hurt and powerless my mom felt because of Dad's cheating—it was all too much to bear! I won't allow anyone to hurt me the way Dad hurt Mom. I just can't give John my whole heart. He might do the same thing that my dad did. I just can't take the chance!"

June defined herself as a person who could occasionally connect emotionally and physically to her significant other, but she could not give her whole heart to anyone out of fear of getting hurt. What she could not see was how her brokenness affected her thinking about marriage relationships. In addition, her choices were modeling an unhealthy pattern to her young daughter.

As we started to examine June's beliefs, she began to see how she really viewed marriage. Her view was clouded by pessimism and thoughts that marriage was an institution where people live miserable-forever-after lives. In her counseling work, she learned how to apply a biblical view of commitment and relationships.

God's best for her (and for all of us) is to encourage the establishment of a committed, intimate, and connected relationship. At first, June tried to rationalize. "Well, I don't know about God's best," she said, "but I know that He understands my heart. He knows what I've been through and how it is just too difficult to even consider marriage."

June had firmly convinced herself that she was acting to protect herself from the kind of hurt and pain she had seen her mother live with for so many years. She did not see her relationship with John as a wonderful partnership between two people who share a gift of love, living as life partners who are connected spiritually, emotionally, and physically.

June admitted that she had not seen many loving relationships in her lifetime. She had been a member of a church for only two years, and the only loving relationship that she could see modeled was her pastor and his wife, a relationship she viewed from a distance.

The good news about June is that she was open and teachable and wanted something better and different in her life. By the time she left counseling, she was entertaining the thought that she could see herself taking the risk of giving her whole heart to John. Additionally, a key to her growth was that she was learning about God's love. Once she experienced God's love for herself—that it was personal, powerful, and unconditional, she began to develop the courage and faith to love others in more unconditional ways than she knew in the past.

Healthy Relationships Require Transparency and Risk

There is a significant truth principle we can glean from the above-mentioned story. Some of us have come from such brokenness that we are always in the self-protection mode. Yet, Jesus clearly models a life of transparency and vulnerability in the area of relationships. He knew Peter would deny Him three times, yet He loved on Peter and gave him a significant assignment to build the kingdom. Jesus knew Judas would betray Him, but He still modeled truth and integrity before Judas and allowed him to stay close until Jesus' time had come to go to the cross. He could have said to both of them, "I know what you both are going to do to hurt me, so I don't want anything to do with you." Yet, He modeled grace for them so that they could benefit. Peter did benefit from the lesson; Judas did not.

Generational Patterns Modeled

Tom came to me desperate to save his marriage after his wife had put her foot down and insisted that either Tom change his cheating ways or she would get a divorce.

"I'm desperate to save my marriage. My wife is going to leave me if I don't get help."

"So, how long have you been cheating"? I asked.

"Well, for the last ten years I've stepped out on my wife."

"Was it a long-term relationship or were you paying for sex?"

"I was paying for sex."

"How long have you been married?"

"Twenty-two years."

"Are you unhappy in your marriage?"

"No, but my wife does not like sex as much as I do."

"Are you trying to connect with your wife in other ways, so that she might be more available to you physically?" I asked.

Tom shook his head. "No, I'm learning that I don't know how to connect in emotional ways. I think I'm a lot like my dad. He did not deal with his emotions. He just took off with his secretary when I was ten years old. He moved on without an apology or anything to start another family."

"How did you feel about that?"

"Not good. Mom was always angry that he left and had other children. My brother and I always felt as though we were in the middle, trying to protect Mom's feelings and also trying to get love from our dad."

"Do you use pornography?"

"Yes, since I was eleven years old."

"How did you start using?"

"I found the magazines in my dad's closet when we went on our visits with him."

"So, how serious are you about your commitment to your marriage?"

"I am very serious. I felt so terribly guilty after each use and was relieved when I got caught. I know that the Lord does not want me to live this way."

Tom's history revealed that his parents had divorced when he was very young due to his father's unfaithfulness. Infidelity seemed to be an accepted practice among the male members of his family. He had grown up in a family where his uncles' cheating on their wives had been tolerated and openly discussed within earshot of the kids. In other words, the belief that cheating on one's wife was acceptable had been modeled and passed down from one generation to the next.

Tom had a serious sexual addiction problem and needed a recovery program for people who used sex as a way to replace real intimacy. He joined a recovery program for men with sexual intimacy issues and began to work on them. After three years of being committed to recovery, Tom came back in with his wife.

"So, Tom, how are you doing?" I asked.

"I'm taking a day at a time, but I had to learn that I was so programmed to engage in destructive habits, that I did not really know how to get out of my addiction. Having godly men in my life has given me permission to look at myself."

Amazingly, Tom's wife had been praying for him for a long time. Although his wife had forgiven him, she had to set some serious boundaries in their relationship. Tom had to agree not to use the Internet without a filter (at home and at work) and to block all the movie channels from cable TV. He also had a male accountability partner who helped him with his addiction issues.

"So how do you think he is doing?" I asked, motioning to his wife.

"Well, I started seeing a real transformation in him about a year ago."

"And what do you attribute that to?"

Tom chimed in. "I've surrendered my heart to the Lord. He is really teaching me how to be a better person and a husband through godly men who have been mentoring me. I could have lost everything as a result of my choices, but looking back, I can see that God was trying to get my attention. God is opening my eyes to who He really is, and I am seeing His love toward me for the first time. I always thought that God was like my earthly dad, punitive and controlling."

Tom is now channeling the energy he was putting into his addiction into cultivating a closer relationship with the Lord and with his wife, which keeps moving their marriage in a positive direction.

A discussion of real intimacy is appropriate here to distinguish it from the false intimacy that is illustrated in the above-mentioned story. Real intimacy is defined as a deep connection with another person on three levels: spiritually, emotionally, and physically. The spiritual component is a way of acknowledging that we are made in the image of God, open to having a personal relationship with Christ. When we are in a relationship with another individual, we are able to respect and acknowledge the spiritual nature that is a part of all of us, calling us to value all people, as all people are made in the image of God. The spiritual part of a person connects to the core of an individual, their heart. When our human spirit is connected to the Spirit of God, we can develop the capacity to love unconditionally the way that God loves us. Emotional intimacy is defined as the ability to connect with others by sharing ideas, thoughts, feelings, goals, and dreams. Emotional intimacy involves our mind, our will, and our emotions. It encompasses the ability to take risks, be transparent, and vulnerable. Physical intimacy is the icing on the cake. We are designed by God as sexual beings, and as such, we have the capacity to enjoy and embrace and express our sexuality in an intimate committed and connected relationship. According to God's biblical standard, the foundations of both spiritual and emotional intimacy should be established before enjoying physical intimacy, as those foundations provide the building blocks for a lasting relationship.

Tom's story above gives us a great biblical insight into how cultivating good habits leads to living in freedom. It takes time to develop new habits, but one must practice intentionality on a daily basis in order to achieve the freedom from an addictive lifestyle. Staying free requires paying attention to the triggers that occur and can cause one to continue in an addictive lifestyle. Triggers often occur automatically and if we give into them, we can find ourselves right back in the lifestyle we were trying to avoid. Here are some additional examples:

Struggle with Addiction

Jan had been free from using cocaine for many years when all of a sudden, she was driving on the highway and a memory came to her of the place where she formerly purchased drugs. The memory was so strong that she turned the car around and started driving in that direction. Then she began to remember and value how much work she had accomplished to achieve her sobriety. There was a definite mental and emotional struggle, until she remembered not just the "high" that she had experienced, giving her a few moments of relief from her difficulties, but also the tremendous pain and devastation that had resulted in a suspended license, broken relationships, lost employment, and the difficulty of starting over.

Ty and Mae

Ty's birth mother had not been able to care for him, so she gave him over to the state when he was five. She was not only neglectful, but always chose the men in her life over her own children. Ty was placed in foster care. The woman who raised him was mean-spirited and abusive, both physically and verbally. When he was twelve, Ty was sent back to live with his birth mom, who by then already had five other children by three different men. She was remarried, and her husband (Ty's step-dad) was a good provider, but favored his birth children and was not emotionally present for Ty.

When Ty grew up and had his own family, he repeated some of the same patterns that had occurred in his childhood, even though he vowed not to do so. He married Mae, a woman who already had children, and he was not emotionally present for his stepchildren. The anger, pain, and distrust of women within him prevented him from having the kind of marriage that he truly desired. Even more difficult was that while he was aware of the damaging effects of his past, he was not aware of how his mistrust of women was damaging his relationship with his wife. He was extremely suspicious and possessive of her, and he constantly accused her of being unfaithful, even though she was faithful to him. The wounded spirit and pain caused by his birth mom kept Ty from really trusting his wife and prevented him from engaging in healthy emotional intimacy. It was after an incident that occurred one evening, when Ty and Mae had gone out to dinner with friends to celebrate their anniversary, that the couple ended up at my office seeking help.

"Every time we go out with friends, Ty accuses me of flirting with the other men in the group, and we end up fighting and spoiling what could have been a wonderful evening. I'm just sick of it," Mae said.

It became clear to me that no matter how much attention Mae gave Ty when they were out with friends, it wasn't enough for him. The arguments Ty and his wife had that developed as a result of Ty's insecurities created hurt feelings and division between them.

"So, tell the counselor the truth, Mae. You were really looking at my friend Ed."

"No, I wasn't," Mae chimed in. "And if you don't deal with these trust issues that you have, we are going to continue to have division in our marriage. You constantly stir up unnecessary conflict, and I am tired of it."

It took time and a lot of work on Ty's part to see how his perception of Mae's behavior in social situations was clouded and distorted due to what had happened to him as a child. Ty shared one incident that happened after he went back to live with his birth mom (at a time she was separated from his step-dad) when she began to bring men into the house to sleep with her. "I remember one night mom brought this guy home. He thought the kids were sleeping and so he stayed the night. I got up in the middle of the night to get something to eat, and I heard sounds coming from Mom's bedroom. I thought she was being hurt. I was really scared, angry, and disgusted, and wanted to help her. After this incident, I remember Mom bringing other men home more often than I care to remember. She even left us with a couple of her boyfriends when she went to work, and both of them treated us badly."

Ty finally began to make the connections between his trust issues with his mom and his relationship with his wife. He became more effective at managing the negative thoughts that bombarded him when a triggering event happened. He could finally see how his past affected his thinking. In counseling, he was developing tools to deal with his own insecurities. He began to see that his wife was different from his mom, and he could learn to trust again. He had to ask God to open his eyes and his understanding so he could see truth clearly. The truth was that he was powerless when he was a kid to change anything, and he had been affected negatively by his past. However, as an adult, he was not powerless. As he talked about the pain and anger that he felt when he was a child and how it all affected him, he began to understand more about his anger and how it affected his relationship with Mae. As he started looking at the issue of forgiveness, he began to more clearly see that the issues with his wife were very different and separate from the issues that he had with his mom. Once aware, he could invite God into his situation to help him to see clearly and not overreact when his trust issues were triggered.

As he began to change, Mae responded more positively to him. He began to experience the kind of intimacy that he longed for. This occurred through awareness, process, and practice.

Awareness of our Life Patterns Increases our Ability to Develop Healthy Perspectives

Learning to make connections from the past helps to heal our brokenness. Half the battle is learning to see truth from a healthy perspective. Seeing from a healthy perspective means being able to separate the lies that we believe from the truth about what is really going on in a relationship. Our negative emotions and woundedness from our past can get in the way of establishing healthy relationships in the present. Being aware of our brokenness gives us insight into current behaviors and patterns. Once an awareness of these patterns develops, we have an opportunity to implement some positive changes.

Looking Within: Becoming Introspective

The good news for the people in the previous stories, and many others like them, is that the negative cycles that caused the pain and unhappiness in their lives don't have to be repeated. By using some of the tools that are outlined below, we can achieve victory over our past and build a positive future for ourselves and our children. In Figure 2 on the following page is a chart outlining some anger management principles.

Listed below are some principles for thoughtful reflection that summarize the chapter:

1. Manage stress effectively by learning to process and then let go of negative emotions such as anger or unforgiveness.

2. Manage stress by setting healthy boundaries in your relationships and not overcommitting to too many events, tasks, or people.

3. Learn, accept, and surrender to God's unconditional love and care toward you. Reframe your thinking with the truth that God

loves you and has a plan and purpose for your life when you are submitted to Him.

4. Cultivate and model good habits that lead to living free. Sometimes this requires letting go of your current lifestyle and changing or adopting new lifestyle choices.

5. Be aware of past triggers from painful life situations, as they can affect current relationships.

6. Ask God to show you how much you are loved unconditionally by Him, and then ask Him to help you to love others in unconditional ways.

Figure 2: Principles for Managing Anger

Prov. 29:11 (NIV)- A fool gives full vent to his anger, but a wise man keeps himself under control.

1. Be aware of and admit your anger.
2. Give your anger creative and healthy expression through exercise, journaling, drawing, painting, talking with a safe person, counseling, role-playing, music, etc.
3. Surrender the control of your anger to God.
4. Take a good look at what might be triggering your anger. Let a counselor help you.
5. Processing anger issues takes time.
6. Determine if your anger is destructive or constructive.
7. Destructive anger can turn into verbal, emotional, or physical abuse that is hurtful to yourself and others.
8. Repressed anger can cause physical illness.
9. Constructive anger can empower action and positive change toward more effective communication.
10. Be aware of defense mechanisms such as the projection of blame at others.
11. Learn to be humble instead of proud.
12. Sometimes low esteem or past hurts can hinder an accurate perception of a situation. Make sure to clarify the intended meaning of what is being communicated.
13. Practice kindness; remember that a soft answer turns away anger.
14. To diffuse a volatile situation, speak more softly than the offending person.
15. Use non-threatening body language to calm a situation.
16. Take full responsibility for your angry actions.
17. Work through old wounds in order to understand why your "buttons" are so easily triggered.
18. Don't let your "buttons" get pushed; take time to regain composure, if necessary.
19. Remember that no one makes you angry; your response is a choice.
20. Communicate by paraphrasing what you have just heard.
21. Focus on issues rather than emotions.
22. Be a role - model of positive behaviors.

CHAPTER 4

Generational Patterns

GOD, a God of mercy and grace, endlessly patient—so much love, so deeply true—loyal in love for a thousand generations, forgiving iniquity, rebellion, and sin. Still, he doesn't ignore sin. He holds sons and grandsons responsible for a father's sins to the third and even fourth generation.
—EXODUS 34:6-7 (MSG)

W hen I was about to deliver my first child, my husband was in the room with me as my labor coach. The doctor had a heart monitor hooked up to me and another one hooked up to the baby. My husband could tell when I was getting ready to have a contraction because he could read the tape coming out of the machine. What he did not realize was that he did not have to tell me that a contraction was occurring. I was already experiencing it intensely before he could get the words out of his mouth.

Deep Brokenness

I offer this illustration because in my clinical work of almost thirty years, I've had the privilege of seeing the inner workings of the lives of many of my patients and experiencing the pain and brokenness that came from their wounded hearts. Sometimes the pain was buried so deep that they didn't know what was happening.

It takes a lot of work searching deep inside our souls and psyches to figure out the causes of pain. Unlike the pain of childbirth, which usually has a happy ending (and we forget about it once we hold that little bundle of joy in our arms), the pain of deep hurts caused by generational patterns can continue to hurt us and those around us for years.

Matt's story

Matt was the third generation male descendant of a father and grandfather who had a history of extra-marital affairs. He dealt with the same challenge in his marriage and faced divorce. As he continued to tell me his life story during our sessions, I began to understand why he was making destructive choices.

"My dad used to take me to bars when I was young. He would always have a girlfriend around. Once I caught him making out with some strange woman at his work. When I confronted him about it, he told me that it was no big thing. He said that as long as he took care of the family, he could have a little extra curricular action on the side. At ten, I really did not understand what 'extracurricular action' meant, but as I grew older, I understood. I used to think that my mom was doing something wrong in the relationship, and I often blamed her for dad's affairs."

"When you take a look at your history, do you see any connections or patterns that you may be repeating in your marriage?" I asked.

Matt acknowledged that he was engaging in very similar patterns his dad had modeled. As we continued working, he could see that many of his actions were tied to what he believed about marriage. "None of my male relatives have been faithful to their wives. I don't think we were meant to be monogamous."

"So, then, why did you get married?"

"I guess I really wanted a family."

As I challenged how he believed, he began to see that his beliefs and actions from his background really affected his present actions. As a new Christian, he went to church most Sundays, but had a difficult time adopting a godly view of marriage. He almost felt that something would be taken away from him if he pursued God's definition of a committed, monogamous relationship. All that he had seen modeled in his life were men living a lifestyle of uncommitted, unfulfilled, and disconnected relationships with a lot of sex. Matt eventually got a divorce and adopted this lifestyle as well.

His situation reminded me of the story in Scripture where Jesus told the rich man to give up everything he had to follow Him. The rich man couldn't let go of his lifestyle. The same was the case with Matt. He thought that it was too difficult to learn the tools to have a godly marriage, so he walked away, just like the rich man. In both instances, these men did not realize that Jesus wanted to add so much more to their lives, if they would just submit to Him. Let's look at this story from Mark 10:17-22 (MSG):

> As he went out into the street, a man came running up, greeted him with great reverence, and asked, "Good Teacher, what must I do to get eternal life?" Jesus said, "Why are you calling me good? No one is good, only God. You know the commandments: Don't murder, don't commit adultery, don't steal, don't lie, don't cheat, honor your father and mother." He said, "Teacher, I have—from my youth—kept them all!" Jesus looked him hard in the eye—and loved him! He said, "There's one thing left: Go sell whatever you own and give it to the poor. All your wealth will then be heavenly wealth. And come follow

me." The man's face clouded over. This was the last thing he expected to hear, and he walked off with a heavy heart. He was holding on tight to a lot of things, and not about to let go.

And the promise of a more abundant life in Mark 10:29-31 (MSG):

> Jesus said, "Mark my words, no one who sacrifices house, brothers, sisters, mother, father, children, land—whatever—because of me and the Message will lose out. They'll get it all back, but multiplied many times in homes, brothers, sisters, mothers, children, and land—but also in troubles. And then the bonus of eternal life! This is once again the Great Reversal: Many who are first will end up last, and the last first."

Wil and Jacquie Chevalier, international communicators and authors of more than fourteen books on relationships, define a godly view of marriage in their marriage study series *More Than Love, the Divine Blueprint* this way: "Marriage is not a social convenience for living together. It is a pattern for living established by God even before man's rebellion and fall. The holiness and perfection of marriage is emphasized by the fact that it was instituted by God before man sinned. 'For this cause a man shall leave his father and mother, and shall cleave to his wife; and they shall become one flesh. And the man and his wife were both naked and were not ashamed.' (Genesis 2:24, 25)

Husband and wife are now united in their life on earth and have the capacity to:

1. Mirror God's image (Genesis 1:27)
2. Multiply a godly heritage (Genesis 1:28)
3. Manage God's realm (Genesis 1:28b)
4. Mutually complete each other (Genesis 2:20-23)"

They also write in their work, *Embracing the Mystery of Love and Marriage*, "The Bible is more than an ancient document detailing God's acts in the past. The Word of God is a vital, up-to-date guidebook on how to live life fully and abundantly right now. God not only created us, He gave us an instruction manual on how to make things work both for His glory and for our success. We need to discover God's way—a way that makes the marriage relationship one of joy, fulfillment, and true happiness."

If Matt in the above-mentioned story had embraced a godly view of the marriage relationship, there still may have been hope for his marriage not to end in divorce. The good news is that with knowledge, understanding, and new and different tools, negative cycles don't have to repeat. God's Word illustrates this truth in Deuteronomy 30:15 (NLT): "Now listen! Today I am giving you a choice between life and death, between prosperity and disaster. For I command you this day to love the LORD your God and to keep his commands, decrees, and regulations by walking in his ways. If you do this, you will live and multiply, and the LORD your God will bless you and the land you are about to enter and occupy."

Choosing life is easier said than done, because it means learning to adopt new beliefs and values that are different from what is familiar.

Exodus 20:4-6 (NIV) reveals how patterns can be continually repeated throughout the generations unless we adopt higher standards and then apply them to our lives: "You shall not make for yourself an idol in the form of anything in heaven above or on the earth beneath or in the waters below. You shall not bow down to them or worship them; for I, the LORD your God, am a jealous God, punishing the children for the sin of the fathers to the third and fourth generation of those who hate me, but showing love to a thousand generations of those who love me and keep my commandments."

Grace Abounds

Scripture often shows where negative generational patterns have been repeated. And even though they repeat, God's grace and mercy cover a multitude of sins. Do you remember the story in the Bible where both Abraham and his son Isaac pretended that their wives were their sisters? Abraham first caused this deception and Isaac repeated his dad's pattern of lying and deceiving many years later. Both were not so unlike us today; when they came up against difficult circumstances, they took matters into their own hands. Both father and son pretended that their wives were their sisters when they thought it would benefit them.

Because of God's grace and intervention, they both were spared the consequences of this deception. That alone is good news for us—that even though we make mistakes and bad choices, God is still protecting us. Let's look at the story in Genesis 20:1-3 (NIV): "Now Abraham moved on from there into the region of the Negev and lived between Kadesh and Shur. For a while he stayed in Gerar, and there Abraham said of his wife Sarah, 'She is my sister.' Then Abimelech king of Gerar sent for Sarah and took her. But God came to Abimelech in a dream one night and said to him. 'You are as good as dead because of the woman you have taken; she is a married woman.'"

Genesis 26:7 (NIV) tells how Abraham's son Isaac repeated a very similar pattern. "When the men of that place asked him about his wife, he said, 'She is my sister,' because he was afraid to say, 'She is my wife.' He thought, 'The men of this place might kill me on account of Rebekah, because she is beautiful.'" Do you think the son, Isaac, inherited his father's ability to deceive, or did his father, Abraham, model a lifestyle of certain values and beliefs that left a powerful impression on him? It is my experience and belief that modeling and lifestyle leave a powerful imprint.

Now, let's look at King David's life. The chart in Figure 3 at the end of this chapter is a genogram of David's family history. This chart paints a picture of David's family tree and some of the consequences of the choices he made, which in turn were passed down to his sons, showing the negative generational cycles that occurred. Sexual sin was introduced in David's life when he committed adultery with Bathsheba. Look at the passage from 2 Sam 11:2-4 (NIV): "One evening David got up from his bed and walked around on the roof of the palace. From the roof he saw a woman bathing. The woman was very beautiful, and David sent someone to find out about her. The man said, 'Isn't this Bathsheba, the daughter of Eliam and the wife of Uriah the Hittite?' Then David sent messengers to get her. She came to him, and he slept with her."

As we look at David's genogram, we see the sexual transgression of adultery is repeated and multiplied in the next generation to include even more unacceptable behaviors when David's son Amnon rapes his half-sister Tamar. Let's examine the story told in 2 Samuel 13:9-15 (NIV):

> "Send everyone out of here," Amnon said. So everyone left him. Then Amnon said to Tamar, "Bring the food here into my bedroom so I may eat from your hand." And Tamar took the bread she had prepared and brought it to her brother Amnon in his bedroom. But when she took it to him to eat, he grabbed her and said, "Come to bed with me, my sister." "Don't, my brother!" she said to him. "Don't force me. Such a thing should not be done in Israel! Don't do this wicked thing. What about me? Where could I get rid of my disgrace? And what about you? You would be like one of the wicked fools in Israel. Please speak to the king; he will not keep me from being married to you." But he refused to listen to her, and since he was

stronger than she, he raped her. Then Amnon hated her with intense hatred. In fact, he hated her more than he had loved her. Amnon said to her, "Get up and get out!"

Another pattern that we see in this genogram is a passive-aggressive behavioral style of both David and his son Amnon. The Bible says that when David found out that his son had raped his daughter, he was furious, and although he displayed the emotion of anger, no additional action was taken. Perhaps David did not take action because he was dealing with guilt resulting from his own choices. We don't know this for sure; but whatever the reason, his lack of action resulted in consequences that were even more devastating. His other son Absalom, Tamar's biological brother, pretended for two years that everything was okay. But the seed of hate and the desire for revenge had been planted in his heart. He did not rest until he plotted to have his brother Amnon murdered.

Interestingly enough, David engaged in a similar type of deception and cover up when he instructed his commander, Joab, to put Bathsheba's husband on the front line of battle and then remove protection from him so that he would be killed in combat. This was done in an effort to cover up David's transgression with Bathsheba, and not surprisingly, a similar deception was committed by David's son Adonijah, when he tried to secure the throne that was meant for Solomon (David and Bathsheba's son.) Does this sound really ugly? I am sure that it does. But if we look at some of the patterns from our own families, we may see things we have done that have been destructive to our children and to our legacy as well. The blessing of this is that the Lord is such a lover of our souls, and He is constantly wooing us to make better choices. He is such a God of grace and mercy.

At the end of David's life, God still said that David was a man after His own heart. (See 1 Samuel 13:14.) This is good news in that it shows us God's unlimited mercy. Even though we make many mistakes, there is always room for recovery, forgiveness, freedom, and change. Also, although David made mistakes as we all do, he always seemed to desire to make corrections when he saw the error of his ways. He was coachable and teachable and wanted to have a right relationship with God.

Implications of Cultural Practices

Another pattern in David's day that had multiple generational implications to both individuals and the nation was the cultural acceptance of having more than one wife. We see this repeated to a greater extent in the generation of David's son Solomon. He had over 700 wives and concubines. The Bible says that these foreign women eventually turned Solomon's heart away from the Lord. Solomon was once considered the wisest man alive. But eventually, he allowed many foreign women, who did not follow the true God, to divide his heart. It is a sad commentary that Solomon's divided heart affected the next generation of descendants as well as a nation.

Solomon began by doing great things. He built and dedicated the temple as a place for God's name to dwell and where His presence and character would be evident. God appeared to Solomon twice and gave him instructions. Solomon, following in the footsteps of his father, David, fully committed himself to God's principles. As a king, he encouraged godly practices among his people and motivated them to give their whole heart to Him. However, as Solomon grew older he came under the influence of his foreign wives and led others to false gods.

"As Solomon grew old, his wives turned his heart after other gods, and his heart was not fully devoted to the LORD his God, as the heart of David his father had been. He followed Ashtoreth the goddess of the Sidonians, and Molech the detestable god of the Ammonites.

So Solomon did evil in the eyes of the LORD; he did not follow the LORD completely, as David his father had done." (1 Kings 11:4 NIV)

Solomon's life shows us some great lessons. Even though he may have had a great model to follow in his father, David, Solomon made his own choices. Solomon still believed in God, but he also allowed the culture of the day to influence him to embrace other gods. In our culture today, we also have issues that influence us and sometimes cause us to avoid doing the right thing.

Listed below are some principles for thoughtful reflection that summarize the chapter:

1. Be aware of the patterns in your own life, both negative and positive.

2. Have the courage to adopt new beliefs and values that are different from what is familiar.

3. Don't allow the cultural influences of our day to turn you away from what is right for your life and circumstances.

Figure 3: Repeated Generational Patterns of David

- Wise man after God's own heart
- Multiple wives
- Abuse of power/authority
- Lust / Sexual issues
- Considerable loss of life, authority, prestige and vitality
- Ambitious

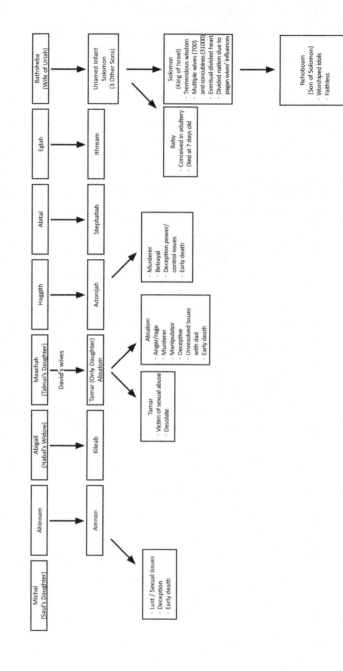

CHAPTER 5

Taking Charge and Overcoming Denial

Above all else, guard your heart, for it is the wellspring of life!
—PROVERBS 4:23 (NIV)

"It's not my fault! It's not my fault, I tell you! He provoked me to anger because of his razor-sharp tongue." "If she had only listened to me, I wouldn't of hit her!" "I only drink because I lost my job." "It's just a small debt. After all, life is short and I need to have a little fun." "Yes, I know he is married, but sometimes I get lonely, and he helps me pay my bills." "I can stop any time I want. Besides, I only watch porn when I'm stressed or angry."

Do any of these statements sound familiar? Can you think of a time when you have rationalized or minimized destructive patterns? You are not alone. The above statements are examples of how all of us can use excuses to ignore or minimize things that may not be healthy for us so that we can continue to engage in them.

Samson, one of the leaders of Israel in the book of Judges, was a perfect illustration of someone who rationalized and minimized destructive patterns. He was born as a Nazirite, set apart to God from birth. God had big plans for him, just as he does for us! Samson's life purpose was to begin the deliverance of Israel from the tyranny of the Philistines. God had given him a special gift of tremendous physical strength. Since he was set apart to God, his Nazirite vow included staying away from eating anything unclean and not cutting his hair. Nevertheless, he developed a passion and a pattern of connecting with pagan women, which caused him to compromise his Nazirite vow. After falling in love with a pagan woman named Delilah, his downfall began. Initially, he thought he was in control. It began with innocent flirtation, but it eventually became very serious. Let's follow the dialogue from Judges 16:6-12 (NIV).

> So Delilah said to Samson, "Tell me the secret of your great strength and how you can be tied up and subdued." Samson answered her, "If anyone ties me with seven fresh bowstrings that have not been dried, I'll become as weak as any other man." Then the rulers of the Philistines brought her seven fresh bowstrings that had not been dried, and she tied him with them. With men hidden in the room, she called to him, "Samson, the Philistines are upon you!" But he snapped the bowstrings as easily as a piece of string snaps when it comes close to a flame. So the secret of his strength was not discovered. Then Delilah said to Samson, "You have made a fool of me; you lied to me. Come now, tell me how you can be tied." He said, "If anyone ties me securely with new ropes that have never even used, I'll become as weak as any other man." So Delilah took new ropes and tied him with them. Then, with men hidden in the room, she called to him, "Samson, the Philistines are upon

you!" But he snapped the ropes off his arms as if they were threads.

Delilah pushed and prodded for an answer and used manipulation and her feminine charms to finally get Samson to tell her the secret to his strength. One would think that Samson would get wise to Delilah's motivation. Samson should have known that this woman would betray him, since the same scenario happened four times. Often, when we are engaged in destructive patterns, we are so comfortable in the situation that we don't see the danger that may lie before us.

Once Samson told Delilah the true secret of his great strength, his enemies descended upon him and seized him, gouged out his eyes, and took him down to Gaza to work as a laborer. You might say to yourself, what a sad story! Ultimately, God restored him by giving him his strength back and allowing him to defeat the Philistines. But this was his final act of courage. He died during this event.

The first step in any recovery program is to admit that there is a problem. Most recovery programs start with the premise that the individual must accept responsibility for his or her actions. The first step in the successful 12-step program of Alcoholics Anonymous tells its participants to admit and surrender. Denial is a main reason it is so difficult for a person to admit that he or she has a problem. Denial indicates an unwillingness to face the truth about ourselves. It is used in psychology to mean an unconscious defense mechanism used to reduce anxiety by denying thoughts, feelings, or facts that are consciously intolerable.

Jay and Mara

Jay's story is a perfect illustration of someone living in denial. He had come to see me with his wife, Mara, after an incident at his work forced him into mandated counseling. Also, his wife started going to a small group at church on addiction and recovery, and her eyes were opened to seeing the truth about her own need to establish boundaries with Jay related to his drinking.

"So, do you have a drinking problem?" I asked, after listening to Jay tell me why he was in my office.

"No," Jay responded, "not at all."

I asked him, "How many beers do you have in the evening after work?"

"Well," Jay reluctantly stated, "only six, most of the time."

His wife chimed in. "Jay, come on! If we are coming here asking for help, why don't you be truthful? You know you drink more than six cans every night!"

"Well," Jay retorted, "I go to work every day and pay the house payment, so the beer is not a problem. I am a good provider and the alcohol does not get in the way of my being able to function."

Mara sighed. "Well, Jay, what about the times I've had to call your work for you because you were too hung over to go in?"

"That was really not the case. I was just sick. Besides," he added, "that only happened two or three times."

Jay came from a family where his mom had a serious prescription drug addiction problem, his dad was a social drinker whom he never saw drunk, and his uncles were all alcoholics.

Do you see the denial picture? Until Jay owns up to the fact that he does have a problem, he will not be on the road to freedom and recovery. He will stay broken and hindered from experiencing God's best for his life. His denial is not only affecting his own lack of recovery, it is also affecting his wife and family. His alcohol problem, if it continues, can cause more rippling and devastating effects for his family, i.e., financial, emotional, and health issues. The person with the problem is the only one who can own it and therefore do something about it.

Denial can be a very blinding thing. We can all rationalize and minimize the behaviors that we want to keep, and avoid issues that we don't want to face. When we avoid our problems, they don't go away, they just get buried for a season. At some point circumstances will arise that force us to deal with them. If we have developed a pattern of avoidance, we have to deal not only with the current stressors that we are facing in our lives, but with the layers of issues that have been buried and are now demanding our attention all at once as well. It is much better to deal with issues once we become aware of a negative pattern or circumstance. Let's look at another case history.

Past Patterns Affecting the Marital Relationship

Maria and Ben came to see me because they were experiencing a great deal of marital discord. After getting some history related to their backgrounds, I discovered that Ben was raised by a dad who was angry much of the time. I soon discovered that Ben related both to his wife and his children as his dad had with him. I observed him being short, terse, rude, and sometimes emotionally abusive during the sessions.

"You are such a witch, and I don't even know why I stay with you!" he screamed during one of the sessions.

Maria responded, "Stop screaming and talking down to me. You always do this at home. That is why it is difficult to hear what you have to say."

After I intervened by calming things down a bit with a time out, I then asked Ben, "Do you think you have an anger problem?"

Ben replied, "No, I don't. She just makes me angry by her actions."

"What actions?" I asked.

"She is pretending to not understand what I am saying."

"Well, do you think you could use your normal voice with a nicer tone to explain what you mean?"

Ben was quiet for a moment. Then he began to speak in a more civil tone. "I was not aware that I was coming across so hard.

I guess my dad talked to me and my sisters and brothers harshly, and I vowed that I would never be that way. I don't want to turn into my dad."

It wasn't until Ben realized that the patterns that he learned from his dad were affecting his current actions with his own family that he became conscious of the reasons he acted the way he did. What he learned was that if he continued to engage in these unhealthy communication patterns, it would be impossible to promote intimacy and connection with his family, something that he desperately desired. But his anger and angry actions were in the way.

Scripture shows us a good example of denial in the account of King David and the difficult time he had coming to grips with the truth about himself. As we know, David had an adulterous relationship with Bathsheba, Uriah's wife, and then tried to cover it up. David did not immediately confess his sin. After about a year, God sent Nathan the prophet to confront him. God was not at all pleased with what David had done, and sent Nathan to David.

> The Lord sent Nathan to David. When he came to him, he said, "There were two men in a certain town, one rich and the other poor. The rich man had a very large number of sheep and cattle, but the poor man had nothing except one little ewe lamb he had bought. He raised it, and it grew up with him and his children. It shared his food, drank from his cup and even slept in his arms; it was like a daughter to him. Now a traveler came to the rich man, but the rich man refrained from taking one of his own sheep or cattle to prepare a meal for the traveler who had come to him. Instead, he took the ewe lamb that belonged to the poor man and prepared it for the one who had come to him. David burned with anger against the

man and said to Nathan. "As surely as the Lord lives, the man who did this deserves to die! He must pay for that lamb four times over, because he did such a thing and had no pity." Then Nathan said to David, "You are the man!" (2 Samuel 12:1-7 NIV)

Notice that David was in such denial that he became self-righteous. Not until Nathan directly confronted him, telling David that the story was about him, did he realize his sin. Once his eyes were opened to the sin in his life, David could then confess it to God and be forgiven. David fully understood that he served a God of unlimited grace and lovingkindness. Believers can be comforted by the fact that since David's sins were forgiven, theirs can be also.

The message of this story is that the worst offender among God's people can appeal to God for forgiveness, for moral restoration, and for full recovery if he or she comes to God with a broken spirit and contrite heart.

One of the greatest ways to become honest with ourselves is to invite God into our life and situation and ask Him to show us things about ourselves that will help us to grow and become all that he created us to become.

In order to invite God into your life, you have to acknowledge that He paid the ultimate price for you personally by dying on the cross. Jesus died for you so that you can have life, freedom, and real joy. "For God so loved the world, that he gave his only begotten Son, that whosoever believeth in him should not perish, but have everlasting life" (John 3:16 KJV). It is difficult to open your heart to someone you don't know. If you ask Christ to come into your heart, He will begin to show you His great love and the specific, individual purpose that He has for you. Once you can identify with His love toward you, it is much easier to take the step of asking Him to show you things about yourself that will help you to live your best life. Will you ask Him to come into your heart today?

Listed below are some principles for thoughtful reflection that summarize the chapter:

1. Learn to take responsibility for your attitudes and actions. Be aware of how denial keeps you from your purpose and your best life, the life that God intended for you to live. Denial keeps you stuck and holding on to negative patterns from the past.

2. Invite safe people into your life to give you an accurate assessment of how they perceive the way you work through difficult challenges. If these include a trusted mentor, friend, or close family member, he or she will tell you things about yourself that you may not be aware of, but will be beneficial for you to know. Look at it as a positive growth experience that will help you lead a purposeful and productive life.

CHAPTER 6

Learning to Think Differently

For as he thinks within himself, so is he.
—PROVERBS 23:7 (NASB)

T his biblical principle means that what we think determines what we believe, and what we believe often determines what we will do. Sometimes what we do does not lead to our best life, the life that God desires for us. Recovering from broken places involves thinking differently, which requires applying faith, action, and courage.

Sia's Painful Childhood

Sia experienced so much pain in her childhood that she couldn't wait to grow up and get out of her home. By the time she was thirteen, her mother had married and divorced three times, and her home life lacked the nurturing and stability that children crave. As the means to escape her unhappy home, Sia married her high school sweetheart right after her eighteenth birthday, not realizing that she had traded her abusive family situation for an abusive marriage. She was divorced three years later, and by the time she came to see me, she had been married and divorced three times, like her mom.

"I really resented my mom for never staying in a relationship," Sia confessed, "and for putting me through so much torture because of all the violence and abuse I saw during my childhood. She had so many men around after my dad left."

"How old were you when your dad left?" I asked.

"I was eight."

"Did you continue to see your dad?"

"No, I didn't see him again until I was eighteen. In the meantime, Mom had several other marriages. Most of them involved emotionally abusive men."

"Just how were they emotionally abusive?"

Sia thought for a moment, and then replied. "One night my mother's husband came in the house cussing. Mom had dinner on the stove. She'd made chicken and vegetables. Mom had his food all nicely displayed on a plate on the counter. I'll never forget what he said: 'What the devil is this slop?' Then he screamed a profanity and threw the plate on the floor. Mom cringed and tried to calm him down, but he continued to berate and disrespect her. I wanted to scream back at him and tell him to leave us all alone, leave and never return. But I knew I would have to pay if I did.

"Unfortunately, I seem to pick men that are that way too. And my daughter is attached to my ex-husband, who has a similar pattern of verbal abuse. I feel so much guilt, because I never wanted to do to my children what my mom did to me. I think I'm not going to date anyone, because all I seem to attract are unhealthy men who treat me poorly."

Sia seemed to choose men who were very similar to the men her mother chose. They were either unable to make long-term commitments, were unfaithful in the marriage, were emotionally unavailable, and/or physically or emotionally abusive. She agreed to spend some time with me exploring her history and the possible reasons she attracted unhealthy men.

After several months of counseling, Sia was able to see that she was making destructive choices. As she began to look inside herself, she was able to see that she was emotionally broken and that brokenness made her crave attention and affection, which made her attach herself to anyone, just to fill that void. Our dialogues became more open and purposeful.

"I guess I'm finally learning at forty-two years old that I need to value myself," Sia acknowledged. "I've had so many messages from my past that made me feel inadequate."

"What messages did you receive?" I asked.

"My mom would always tell my sisters that they were smart and pretty. I was labeled as a good girl, but not a smart and pretty girl. I received average grades, and I didn't look like the rest of the family. I have a dark complexion that was never validated by my mom. It was a running joke in the family that perhaps I had a different dad because I did not look like my sisters."

"It sounds like you adopted some negative messages about who you are and then acted them out in your life."

"Yes, I don't really think that I know who I am. I've always seen myself as an average-looking person with average intelligence that is less than that of other people. I always conclude that most of the people I know are head and shoulders above me when it comes to looks and intelligence."

"Perhaps that is who you think you are, but have you asked God to show you who you really are?"

"No, I guess I haven't." The quizzical expression on Sia's face told me she didn't fully grasp what I was asking of her.

"Well, let's explore who you are in Christ, and what His design and desires are for your life. The Bible says that you are fearfully and wonderfully made and that you are God's unique work of art, so it will be difficult to compare you with other people. As you begin to value and love yourself, you can start to model that to your daughter. That would be a beginning step in learning to reverse this negative pattern you have adopted."

Sia finally learned that she needed to value and love herself before she was ready to enter into another relationship. Learning to value and love herself involved a process of acquiring new relationship-management tools and realizing that she couldn't do it on her own. Some of those tools were learning how to erase the negative tapes about herself that she had come to believe in, and also beginning to think differently about herself. She also needed to learn about God's unconditional love for her from a new perspective.

Erasing tapes is not an easy process. It requires reprogramming your thinking to see how much you are loved by a God who is both caring and personal. Reprogramming takes time and requires you to look at the current beliefs that are tied to your identity, and then to fight through the negative messages that you have come to believe.

It is difficult to see God as a loving father when earthly parents are critical and rejecting. As Sia proceeded with her counseling, I encouraged her to join Celebrate Recovery, a Christ- centered 12-step program, or find a small group that adheres to sound biblical principles. Through this multi-step study, Sia learned that she could have her relationship needs met while connecting with healthy adults, instead of spending her time and energy in romantic liaisons with unhealthy people who abused her emotionally and physically and left her feeling empty and used. As she experienced the love and care of others through a safe community of both affirmation and accountability, Sia stopped feeling so lonely and saw that she could get her relationship needs met by interacting positively and socially with healthy adults. As a result, Sia was able to realize that although she desired to have a love relationship, she did not have to settle for the choices she had made in the past.

Connecting the Dots

Part of recovering from negative past patterns is to be able to learn to think differently. In the above-mentioned story, Sia had to see herself differently. That took some self-reflection and understanding on her part about what kinds of beliefs and messages she had received and accepted as a child and how those beliefs had manifested in her life as an adult. One such message that Sia believed was: I have to work harder to be accepted by people because I'm not as pretty or smart. Sia admitted that she actually lowered her standards for how she chose potential partners as a result of what she believed about herself.

Replacing negative messages with positive, life-giving messages is a process. If we've had a lifetime of negative programming, it takes some time to learn to erase the tapes. Advertising is a good illustration of this principle. Advertisers write catchy jingles and slogans that play over and over, by design, in order to condition our minds. For example, I still remember some of the advertising for the television shows that I used to watch as a little girl. I used to love the superhero shows Batman and Superman. I can still remember the opening line for Superman. "Look, up in the sky! It's a bird. It's a plane. No, it's Superman!" I'm not actively thinking about this theme, but once in a while, like when a new superhero movie comes along, something may get triggered and that theme will come back into my mind. As young children, we really don't have any control over the negative or positive programming that goes into our hearts and minds. That is why good parenting is so important. However, as we become adults, we do have the responsibility to look at the tapes or scripts that have been part of our lives and have caused us to act in ways that may not lead us to living our best life. Then it becomes our responsibility to automatically reject or believe those thoughts that come into our heads and then our hearts.

Another way of valuing ourselves is to look at our Creator to see how He loves and values us. This requires us to accept how God looks at a life. He says that we are fearfully and wonderfully made. (See Psalm 139:14.) If we humble ourselves long enough to see through God's eyes, our value will start to increase. We *have* to ask God to help us see our value from His perspective, not our own. Sometimes we grow up equating our value with our ability to perform well. God looks at us in a different way. He values what He created—you!

In order to see from His perspective, we have to believe not only that His character is loving, but also that He wants to love us without conditions. Let's look more closely at God's love. "Dear friends, let us love one another, for love comes from God. Everyone who loves has been born of God and knows God. Whoever does not love does not know God, because God is love. This is how God showed his love among us: He sent his one and only Son into the world that we might live through him" (1 John 4:7-9 NIV).

His love is also personal. "'For I know the plans that I have for you,' declares the Lord, 'plans to prosper you and not to harm you, plans to give you a hope and a future'" (Jeremiah 29:11 NIV). Once we are able to accept that God's love is both personal and individual, we can then begin to accept His love. Once we are able to take in and receive his love, it is easier to look at some of the negative, well-worn patterns that have permeated our lives and might be keeping us stuck, hindering us from living our best life.

Trina's story of Generational Codependency

After seeing Trina for a year and watching her make progress with the anxiety that had been plaguing her for a long time, I heard her say during one of our sessions: "I feel as though I'm in a rut. I am beginning to experience a lot of panic feelings again, like I did a year ago. I feel stuck."

"So what do you think brought this on?" I asked.

"Well, two of my girlfriends just got married. I always thought that I would get married before them. I realized all of a sudden that

I am forty years old and still living at home. I was really feeling sad about it and then went to sleep. I woke up in the middle of the night in a panic with my heart racing and finding it difficult to breathe."

"Did you have to go to the hospital?" I asked.

"No, not like I did before. It calmed down after about ten minutes."

After working with Trina for some time, we both began to understand her problem. Although she really wanted to get married, her primary issue was not getting married itself. It was what marriage represented, which was living apart from her family system. Her primary concern was that if that event did not happen, she would stay trapped in her parent's home. Trina had real fears of moving out on her own. She had several tapes in her head that shouted, "You can't make it on your own!" And these tapes had been reinforced by her family.

Trina represented the third generation in a family rife with codependency. Trina's grandmother was a serious enabler, in that she took care of all of her adult children. They were allowed to live with her, and she did all of the cooking and cleaning for them, even though they were not disabled. Trina's mom followed the same patterns helping to rescue her adult siblings every time they were in financial trouble. Now Trina was following the same pattern, and was expected to do so. Trina decided that she was ready to live on her own. However, as soon as she brought it up to her family, the same codependent thinking was reinforced. "You can't make it on your own, you know you have problems with anxiety and you need us." These messages dumped a lot of false guilt onto an already stuck person.

In order to help herself, Trina had to open her eyes to see the negative tapes that she had come to believe in. As she began to see the truth about herself, that she was a capable person and able to live on her own, she had to find the courage to take action steps, even though she was not being supported by her family.

Over time, Trina not only challenged what she believed, but began to take action steps toward independence. She started taking control of her life by getting on an anti-anxiety medication and reframing her thinking. She also started setting healthy boundaries with her family and started moving toward the career goals that could give her more independence and empowerment.

Challenging Beliefs

Thinking differently requires a willingness to challenge what you believe and then take action that you have come to understand to be in your best interest. Trina had to challenge her beliefs about taking medication. She came from a background where she was labeled "crazy and different" by her family for taking anti-anxiety medication. She had to figure out for herself whether this would be a good decision for her by seeking out a professional person she trusted. She also had to find the courage to change her thinking about how to set healthy boundaries with people who were trying to control her.

Blana's story

Blana came in for counseling to look at the past patterns in her life. Looking into her past allowed me to see that most of the women in her family had children out of wedlock and modeled single-parent households. Blana was now married for the second time, but was having challenges in her marriage because of conflict with her husband.

"What is the conflict about?" I asked.

"John wants me to stop working. He wants me to focus on the kids."

"Is that what you want?"

"Well, kind of. It would be nice to stay home and focus my energy on the kids. After all, I've worked hard all of my life and could use a break. But, I like to make my own money. It's hard to trust men. My dad left when I was nine years old."

"Do you see any evidence that your husband is not trustworthy?"

"No, he is wonderful with me and the kids, and a great provider, but I'm just scared. I don't want the same thing to happen to me as it did to my mom."

Blana could not see herself staying at home due to her inability to trust that her husband would remain faithful in his role as a father and husband. She had been wounded so many times before and had heard stories from her mother and grandmother of how their husbands abandoned their marriages. And, of course, she was the product of her own dad leaving when she was just nine years old.

"Do you believe that God wants the best for your life?" I asked.

"Yes."

"Okay, so why don't you invite Him into your decision-making process."

After some time in counseling, Blana developed a new awareness about how she was thinking. She realized that the lifestyle choices that both her mother and grandmother modeled had left a powerful imprint on her. One of the messages she learned growing up was that she needed to be totally independent—not depending on or trusting a man to help her. Early in her life, she vowed to herself that she would be her own person. As a result, when she married the second time, her wounds and modeling were so ingrained in her that she acted out these beliefs in her marriage. She realized that her own brokenness prevented her from being transparent and vulnerable with her spouse.

"I guess I'm seeing that I have walls up in my relationship."

"Tell me more about that."

"Well, I didn't realize it before coming to counseling, but I can see that I get very defensive in a lot of areas. The walls are definitely up."

As we began to work in those areas, Blana began to risk more with her feelings and took small steps in allowing her walls to come down. She could see that the wall of self-protection that she put up against her husband was affecting her family in hurtful ways.

She often said that she was the victim of a generational curse, in that the past three generations were single-parent households with a lot of personal and financial struggles. She would often pray, "Lord, reverse this generational curse!" What she did not expect was that God was answering her prayer by starting with her. He was changing her thinking. Her past thinking contributed to her inability to let go and do something new. That something new would mean staying home and providing emotional security for their four children. She did not even know what that looked like since she grew up in a single-parent home, where she and her three siblings took care of themselves while their mother worked two jobs. She needed to find the courage to acknowledge that what she saw modeled and what she learned in her past were not God's best for her in her present situation.

Moving Forward

God tells us what to think on in the book of Philippians. "Fix your thoughts on what is true, honorable, and right, and pure, and lovely, and admirable. Think about things that are excellent and worthy of praise" (Philippians 4:8 NLT). However, there are so many negative things happening in our world that it is sometimes hard to focus on the good. Even though God's promises are so real, sometimes they are drowned out by the negative circumstances we face.

Truly, if we want our lives to be restored, we have to get back to basics. Basic living means developing a reverential fear of God and learning to adopt His principles for living well. It also means living out our faith—putting it into action. Negative thinking can stop us from living our best life. It can paralyze us and keep us from living the way we were created to live. It is important that we challenge ourselves in how we think. Remember, I said earlier that what we believe affects what we do, and what we do may not lead to our best life. Let's look at the following story.

Pattern of Attracting Unhealthy Relationships

Norm grew up in a home believing that he did not matter. Even though his brothers and sisters were only a few years younger, Norm took care of a lot of their physical and emotional needs. His mom was a single parent, worked two jobs, and relied on Norm to take care of his brothers and sisters. As Norm grew up and got married, the same pattern emerged where he continuously attracted women who took advantage of him. Norm was working on his third marriage.

"My first and second wives kept a lot of secrets. They both left me with a great deal of debt."

"How did they keep secrets?" I asked.

"One had a shopping addiction and just shopped a lot online without my knowledge, and the other would always give money to her family, without my permission."

"Did you try to set up healthy boundaries to stop this in either situation?"

"No, I thought that I was supposed to take care of them and their needs."

As Norm continued in counseling, he began to realize the same pattern that had evolved in his childhood—taking care of his siblings and putting himself last—became part of his pattern throughout his adulthood in his significant relationships. As God opened his eyes and understanding, he began to see the truth about himself, and that he needed to value himself and practice better stewardship over himself and his resources.

Norm had to learn to counteract the negative with the truth about what God said about who he really was. Norm was fearfully and wonderfully made, and not made for abuse. Now it was Norm's responsibility to take more control over his life with God's great help.

God tells us in His Word that the plans that He has for us are good and not evil, to give us a hope and a future (see Jeremiah 29:11). He always has a purpose to restore, heal, and move us toward the goals and dreams that we have inside of us. Those dreams are God inspired, God created, and God directed. Discouragement can get you off track and away from moving toward accomplishing the goals that are purposed in your heart.

Here are a few principles to help you think differently in order to accomplish your goals:

1. *Reframe your thinking.* A few years ago, my husband had a major illness that forced him to retire two years early. At first, we saw this as a great calamity that put a big dark cloud on our future. During retirement, however, my husband had a chance to rest, heal, and begin recovery. It was then that we had a revelation! The big picture began to unfold, and when we began to pray about the situation, we could see God working in our lives and circumstances! It is difficult to be open to future opportunities if we are stuck in our present circumstances.

Two years later, when my husband's recovery was complete, we were able to move to a brand new, slower-paced community seventy miles away that fit right into the purposes that God had for our lives. This book is part of the fruit of that season. Thinking differently caused us to grieve and then let go of the past, accept what was in front of us, and ask God to reveal our next steps, which he did in a grand way. If you can learn to reframe your circumstances, see the good, and grow through the difficulty, then you will continue to move toward the great purpose that God has for your future.

2. *Forgive the past.* Staying stuck with past unforgiveness and

regrets can affect your thinking in negative ways. Unforgiveness invites resentment; resentment invites anger, which can keep you stuck from dreaming new dreams and seeing new opportunities. Don't stay stuck in unforgiveness. It will block your blessings. Here are some steps to help you with forgiving yourself and others.

a. *Own your feelings.* Often, we don't like to admit negative emotions such as anger or resentment. First and foremost, if we want to move past our pain to get all that God has for us, we have to admit that we are struggling with negative emotions such as anger, jealously, resentment, or bitterness.

b. *Talk about your feelings.* Communicate with someone who is safe, such as a pastor, a good friend, or a professional counselor. Talk specifically about the offense and why you are having difficulty letting go of the hurt and pain that the offender caused you. Talking about it will help you to understand yourself and your perspective.

c. *Seek God's help.* Ask God to open your eyes to see how unforgiveness might be affecting you (e.g., staying away from others, isolating, having a sense of mistrust and safety in daily living, misdirected anger, health issues, angry outbursts, panic attacks).

d. *Commit to releasing negative emotions.* Make a pact with yourself and God, before you begin the process, that you want to be able to release these painful feelings so that you can have room to think and move on to more positive life achieving goals.

e. *Confront your pain.* In order to get to the end goal of forgiveness, process your feelings. Talking about past hurts will bring up emotional pain, which in turns brings back old memories. Don't be afraid of the pain. Pain is often a temporary event. "Weeping may endure for a night, but joy comes in the morning" (Psalm 30:5b NKJV).

f. *Actively forgive.* Remember that forgiveness does not necessarily mean reconciliation with the person who offended you or condoning what they did. It is for you to feel better by letting them off your hook and onto God's justice!

g. *Partner with God.* Invite God into your situation to help you to forgive the person who violated you in some way. Some things can only come from God's hand. An example might be a person who was physically or sexually abused as a child. This often has devastating consequences on the victim and can take a lot of recovery work. When working with family genograms, I often find that cycles of abuse can go from generation to generation. Forgiveness is a component of the healing process that can stop this negative generational legacy.

3. *Learn about God's love for you.* God's love is amazing! Growing up as a Roman Catholic and attending Catholic schools in my childhood gave me an understanding of the triune Godhead: the Father, Son, and the Holy Spirit. However, I did not cultivate a personal relationship with the Lord until I became an adult. As I

studied His Word, I learned about a God who desired to establish an intimate relationship with me personally.

I can see both the difficult things that happened as well as the wonderful events that shaped my life. Looking back, I can see God's hand weaving and working in my life to draw me closer to Him. Some of that weaving and working was seeing me through several major illnesses in my life. When I was in first grade, I was diagnosed with rheumatic fever, which could have affected my heart. I could not walk for one year. The doctors indicated that I would be on penicillin until age twenty-one. Miraculously, I was taken off the medication at age fourteen. At seventeen, all of a sudden, I just started bleeding and had to have major surgery to remove a kidney duct. Twenty-one years ago, I had breast cancer and it came back a second time, three years later, in the same breast. This in itself was a miracle in that had it come back in the other breast, we would have been be dealing with a more difficult battle, metastatic breast cancer. Thankfully, the second time around, I had a mastectomy. That was in August of 1997. I have been cancer free ever since!

Listed below are some principles for thoughtful reflection that summarize the chapter:

1. What we believe often determines what we will do.

2. Learn to reframe your circumstances to see the positive things in your life and God at work.

3. Forgive the past with God's help and go through the active process of forgiving.

CHAPTER 7

Magical Thinking—
Reality, Faith,
and the Fight

Surely you desire truth in the inner parts; you
teach me wisdom in the inmost place.
—PSALM 51:6 (NIV)

Life can be a difficult journey. As faith-filled believers, we know that we are not exempt from trials and challenges. The only difference between non-believers and us is that we serve a loving God who can help us navigate the storms of life.

However, there seems to be something I call "magical thinking" among some people who are under the impression that they can just "pray" for problems to go away. Prayer is a powerful tool that avails much. God tells us in Scripture to pray for our needs and also intercede for the needs of others. However, in addition to the faith part of prayer, there is an action part. Scripture tells us in the book of James that faith without works is dead. (See James 2.) Believers often run with the faith part but ignore the part that requires action.

A good illustration of this principle is the first time I worked through breast cancer in 1994. I had several people who cared about me pray for healing in my life. I was very grateful for their prayers. However, I had a friend come up to me and tell me confidently that I would not have to undergo surgery and God would heal me. Even though I desperately wanted to believe my friend, and claim this promise for my life, all of the steps were pointing to surgery and trusting God to work healing in my life through the medical process. If I had listened to that person, I don't think that I would be writing this book today, as I would already be in Heaven! God is Sovereign and can heal through many different means. However, it takes courage and faith to surrender to the process of surgery—even though it would be wonderful to be instantly healed which, by the way, God can and sometimes does! The different ways that Jesus healed others are recorded in the gospels in the New Testament. As you read and study them, you will see that we serve a loving God who desires to heal and restore our lives.

The process I used was prayer, a good surgeon, good nutrition, and follow-up treatments to fight the cancer. The magical thinking would have come into play had I not been willing to submit to the difficult surgery as well as the uncomfortable, painful, and inconvenient healing process that led to my complete recovery. It takes a lot to surrender to the process. All of us would like to get to the destination without any discomfort. And that brings up another discussion about what God may be trying to teach us about the process of healing instead of the destination of healing.

If we are talking about emotional or physical healing, the process may be painful and it may feel like we will never get to the restoration part of the story. But there are a lot of powerful lessons that come from pain. Some of these lessons can include establishing new normals for our lifestyle, reestablishing priorities, valuing significant relationships, not taking our health for granted, and growing closer to God.

A Disneyland God

Many believers fall away from the faith when they feel their prayers are not being answered or when they do not receive whatever it is they are praying for. One such person came in for counseling.

Magical Thinking and Expectations

Nala came to see me in distress saying, "I've done everything that I am supposed to do. I volunteer at church to help others. I pray daily, and God still does not answer my prayer. I am so discouraged that I just want to give up."

"How is it that God has not answered your prayers?" I asked.

"Well, for one thing, he has not sent me a husband. I've been divorced for fifteen years, and I'm still alone, even though I pray to God to send a man into my life."

I responded gently. "Companionship is wonderful, and it is normal for you to want to have a companion and life partner, but having the wrong man in your life is not going to make you happy."

"Yes, other people have told me that, but I still want a husband, and I've done my part!" a petulant Nala responded.

I had to help Nala realize was that she was basing her theology on performance—as if she was working in a business and expected a paycheck for work well done. Nala felt that she had dotted every i and crossed every t as she was supposed to, so why wasn't she getting her "reward"? Why wasn't God answering her request?

If God does not answer Nala's prayers the way that she thinks He should, she gets depressed and feels hopeless. Hopeless people don't have a lot of energy to continue living out their purpose. Discouragement makes people do desperate things, i.e., finding an emotionally unavailable person to meet their needs, settling for less than what they deserve. Desperation is a recipe for disaster in every human situation; and the lesson here is that Nala should pray for God's will to be done in her life.

When our definition of what is supposed to happen doesn't, we sometimes take matters into our own hands. Abraham and Sarah are a perfect example of this kind of thinking.

God promised Abraham that his seed would continue on, and Sarah assumed that she was too old for that to happen. So, she took matters in her own hands. She told Abraham to sleep with her handmaiden, Hagar, and have a child by her. Genesis 16:1-2 (MSG) says: "Sara, Abraham's wife, hadn't yet produced a child. She had an Egyptian maid named Hagar. Sara said to Abraham, 'God has not seen fit to let me have a child. Sleep with my maid. Maybe I can get a family from her.' Abraham agreed to do what Sara said."

Well, you know the mess that was created by this scenario. Once the child, Ishmael, was born by Hagar, Sarah became jealous, and Abraham had major marital discord in his life. Abraham had to send Hagar away because of the conflict. Some of the Arab and Israeli conflict that exists today can be traced back to this story.

Oftentimes our desires are filled with a worldly view of what it takes to be happy. Sometimes we are so blinded by addictions or unhealthy lifestyle choices that we are not even in touch with what it would take to live our best life.

Geoff's Pattern of Addiction

Geoff came to me seeking professional help because he was struggling with a lifetime habit of pornography, and his wife had threatened to divorce him if he did not seek counseling. Geoff was first exposed to pornography when he was ten years old. His dad used to watch X-rated movies, and Geoff used to sneak a look from his bedroom. With access to the Internet, porn was so accessible that his habit had escalated out of control and taken over his life.

"Well," he reported, "I don't know why she is complaining. It's gotten a lot better. I used to engage at least five days a week, and now I'm down to three or four days."

"Which is it—three, or four? I asked him.

"Well, probably four," he admitted. Yet, he continued to minimize how his use of porn was affecting his marital relationship. When his wife joined us for the sessions, she revealed that they no longer had a satisfying physical relationship. Most of the time, Geoff became impotent with her. However, he had no problem performing when he was using fantasy material on the Internet or watching a porn movie.

I can tell you that God's best for Geoff and his wife is an intimate, connected relationship with no fantasy ghosts in the middle of their bedroom. God's best is that the marital bed stays undefiled, protected, and valued. However, until Geoff recognizes that this long-standing pattern is destroying him and his relationship, it won't change. As long as he continues to entertain destructive behaviors, he will get deeper into his addiction and further away from a satisfying, authentic, and healthy relationship with his wife.

Another form of magical thinking is the use of engaging in a lot of energy to pray against the negative generational patterns, instead of taking ownership and responsibility for the choices that we have in reversing those patterns.

Joan's story

Joan came in seeking help because of the stress her finances were putting on her relationship. "This is the second home that I have lost, and I really don't know what is going on. Satan is really attacking my finances," were the first words out of her mouth on our first session. "I swear, this is a generational curse," she continued. "I am the first generation to graduate from college and finally land a good job. My parents were poor and we always had to move because my dad always lost jobs."

After talking with her for a considerable period, I asked, "How consistent are you at paying your bills?"

"Well," Joan said, "I always pay late since I'm always playing catch up."

"You stated earlier that you've had a great-paying job for the last ten years. How is it that you are always playing catch up?"

"Last month I took another trip, so I got behind on some of my bills."

"Have you considered going to a financial management class?" I asked.

"No, I know how to manage my money. I have a degree in business," she answered, her tone defensive.

What Joan didn't see was that even though she was educated in the area of business, she had to unlearn some behaviors she had acquired during her formative years while living in a home that lacked good financial habits. It was easier for Joan to be in denial and blame her problems on a generational curse or some evil force than to admit she needed to unlearn some bad habits and replace them with new money-management skills.

Certainly, for the believer, we are in a spiritual battle. Ephesians 6:11(NIV) tells us to "put on the full armor of God so that you can take your stand against the devil's schemes." However, we also have our part to consider. We need tools and an action plan to reverse the negative patterns that have plagued our lives.

Some of these tools include professional counseling, small group work, a 12-step program, fellowship with other believers, establishing mentoring relationships, going back to school, recovery meetings, medication (if necessary), a teachable heart, a willingness to learn new things, personal accountability, and establishing new normals. A new normal is achieved by looking at life differently than how we've viewed it in the past, and then thinking differently and taking action steps. Part of the action steps involve overcoming obstacles that we have feared in our past.

Prayer and Reality Component

Finally, a key to avoiding magical thinking and to living life to the fullest is praying about and living in the present reality of our situation. Part of the difficulty that we have in dealing with issues of pain is that we like to avoid things that are difficult for us to deal with. However, if we live in the reality of our situation and face the truth about it, God can assist us in overcoming obstacles in our lives; but we have to allow Him to do it.

God can make anything possible as long as we can handle the truth, even though it might be painful.

Truth vs. Denial

Marilyn came to see me because she had been in an adulterous marriage for ten years. She admitted that she had been in denial and did not want to face the truth about what was really happening. As long as it was not in front of her face, she could go on living as if everything was okay. She admitted later that on one level she knew her husband was betraying her, but on some subconscious level, she did not want to deal with it.

She had no choice but to come face-to-face with what was happening when a friend saw her husband out with another woman. After confronting him, her husband came clean about having an affair. When Marilyn finally heard the truth from his lips, she had no choice but to awaken from the fantasy world that she had been living in. For years she had been praying, "Lord, teach me the truth about my marriage." Now, after ten years of praying, she finally had the courage to admit that God had answered her prayer. Despite how difficult it was to deal with the truth, she could finally move on with her life. She no longer had to continue in a pretend world that she and her husband were creating. She had to face the truth about what was really going on and then make decisions about what she was going to do. Now she could move toward processing the truth, grieving, and moving forward with her life.

Prayer is a key that opens up the door and invites a loving God into your situation. It is simply communicating to God what is in your heart, and also acknowledging who He is. Sometimes it is difficult to pray if we view God as critical and judgmental of us.

Many years ago, when I was working as an intern, a woman came in to see me who was very distraught over her difficult marriage. As she tried to express her feelings about her relationship, she appeared quite closed and ashamed at the way she was thinking. She appeared to be "stuck" in her emotions, and said to me, "Well, I can't say what I am really feeling and thinking. God might get mad at me."

I responded, "Don't you think that God already knows what is in your heart and what you are thinking anyway? You might just as well confess what you are feeling so that you can move past these negative emotions. God has big shoulders and is able to handle your ugly feelings."

We often put God in a box and act as if He is going to "punish" us for thinking or feeling a certain way. If we were raised with judgmental, condemning, or critical authority figures, we will often see God as a punitive authority figure who wants to punish us if we make a mistake. Once we get to know Jesus, and experience His unconditional love and care toward us, we find out there is real freedom in establishing an authentic relationship with a living God who cares for us and about us.

Prayer is a powerful tool that works! Faith increases, circumstances change, both emotional and physical healing happens, and purpose is established! Prayer also helps us to deal with difficult circumstances that will come into our lives. Asking God to show us wisdom in any given situation gives us the freedom to release the worry and anxiety that we are holding on to.

There are many examples from God's Word showing us how

prayer works. Queen Esther and her staff prayed about how to approach a pagan king. Not only did she receive wisdom, but also her life was spared and her people were victorious (Book of Esther).

King David and his men had just returned from Ziklag and discovered that the Amalekites had taken all their wives and children, as well as their possessions. David's men were so devastated that they started blaming him for what happened. David was faced with a difficult set of circumstances. His followers were thinking about stoning him. His loved ones, as well as the women and children of the men who followed him, had been kidnapped. It is understandable why he starting sinking into depression. However, he knew that he had one place to turn for help, and that was to God. David understood the power of God to work things out for his good, and he trusted His sovereign authority to bring triumph out of tragedy! David would recover all that was lost or stolen. Not only did David recover all of his possessions, but the wives and children were returned unharmed. Here is the story as related in 1 Samuel 30:1-7 (NIV).

> David and his men reached Ziklag on the third day. Now the Amalekites had raided the Negev and Ziklag. They had attacked Ziklag and burned it, and had taken captive the women and all who were in it, both young and old. They killed none of them, but carried them off as they went on their way. When David and his men came to Ziklag, they found it destroyed by fire and their wives and sons and daughters taken captive. So David and his men wept aloud until they had no strength left to weep. David's two wives had been captured—Ahinoam of Jezreel and Abigail, the widow of Nabal of Carmel. David was greatly distressed because the men were talking of stoning him; each one was bitter in spirit because of his sons

and daughters. But David found strength in the Lord his God. Then David said to Abiathar the priest, the son of Ahimelech, "Bring me the ephod." Abiathar brought it to him, and David inquired of the Lord, "Shall I pursue this raiding party? Will I overtake them?" "Pursue them," he answered. "You will certainly overtake them and succeed in the rescue."

The Fight

We all know that evil exists. We are in a spiritual battle. God's Word tells us that we are not only in a spiritual battle, but are to gird ourselves up for it. (See Ephesians 6.) Obviously, if we did not have to struggle with evil, God would not tell us to prepare ourselves. Part of reversing the negative generational patterns in our lives is to put on the full armor of God. Reversing negative patterns means adopting new emotional tapes, discerning truth from lies, living a life of integrity and honesty before others and before God, and being alert to deception that tries to influence us away from God's best. Warren Weirsbe, in his New Testament exposition commentary "BE" series (Victor Books 1996), describes the full armor of God in this way:

"But in a sense, the 'whole armor of God' is a picture of Jesus Christ. Christ is the Truth (John14:6), and He is our righteousness (2 Cor. 5:21) and our peace (Eph. 2:14). His faithfulness makes possible our faith (Gal. 2:20); He is our salvation (Luke 2:30); and He is the Word of God (John 1: 1, 14). This means that when we trusted Christ, we received the armor. Paul told the Romans what do with the armor (Rom. 13:11-14): wake up (Rom. 13:11), cast off sin, *and "put on the armor of light* (Rom. 13:12)."

The good news is that we are not in this spiritual battle by ourselves. We serve a big God who is able to help us on the battlefield of our lives. When I'm in a fight, I visualize the tools necessary to win. This is a combination of a good plan, a belief in a powerful

God, and usually, hard work that requires much perseverance. A great illustration in Scripture is in the story of Nehemiah, who went through many difficulties trying to rebuild the wall of Jerusalem. He felt a great burden to rebuild the wall that was broken down and had been destroyed by fire.

Some of our lives look a lot like that. They have been destroyed by rejection, abandonment, anger, or various addictions. Looking at the circumstances, they may seem hopeless. Yet, God raises up people like Nehemiah who will go, gather a team, and encourage others to teach, heal, and restore. However, restoring that wall was no easy assignment. Evil men used intimidation, discouragement, control, fear tactics, and false accusations to keep him from his purpose. Yet, Nehemiah continued to focus, pray, and take action. Half of the men did the work, and the other half were equipped with spears, shield, bows, and armor. They completed the work in fifty-two days! (See Nehemiah 6:15.) This is a great story of encouragement, illustrating that restoration from hard places is possible and God has a plan, a purpose, and unlimited resources, if a life is submitted to Him.

Another great example of restoration from negative generational cycles is found in the story of the Hebrew people, who experienced generational slavery for about 400 years. God heard their cries for help and raised up Moses to be their deliverer. After fleeing Egypt for killing an Egyptian who was mistreating the Hebrew slaves, he fled to Midian where he lived for forty years. Little did he know that God was preparing him for a new adventure and a huge task! At age eighty, God called him to go back to Egypt and deliver the people from harsh slavery. When he returned, he and his brother, Aaron, went to Pharaoh and told him to let the people go. Not only did Pharaoh *not* let the people go, but also after his first visit with Moses and Aaron, he made things much harder for the people.

"That same day Pharaoh gave this order to the slave drivers and foreman in charge of the people. 'You are no longer to supply the people with straw for making bricks; let them go and gather their own straw. But require them to make the same number of bricks as before, don't reduce the quota. They are lazy; that is why they are crying out, "let us go and sacrifice to our God." Make the work harder for the men so that they keep working and pay no attention to lies.'" (Exodus 5:7-9 NIV)

The principle here is that when we are trying to break a pattern or to make a significant change, it will sometimes get worse before it gets better. The people were angry with Moses for their circumstances. They were so wrapped up in their pain that they did not have the faith to see that freedom was coming. They judged Moses and Aaron harshly for stirring things up with Pharaoh, even though they were praying to get out of their difficult situation.

Exodus 5:19-21 (NIV): "The Israelite foreman realized they were in trouble when they were told, 'You are not to reduce the number of bricks required of you for each day.' When they left Pharaoh, they found Moses and Aaron waiting to meet them, and they said, 'May the Lord look upon you and judge you! You have made us a stench to Pharaoh and his officials and have put a sword in their hand to kill us.'"

Things temporarily got worse for the Israelites, but God still had a powerful plan for their freedom. Thankfully, Moses, even though discouraged at times, continued to practice faith and obedience in God and boldly took the steps to secure their freedom.

CHAPTER 8

Building a Positive Legacy for the Next Generation

One generation shall commend your works to
another, and shall declare your mighty acts.
—PSALM 145:4 (NASB)

Life is difficult. If we can cling to God in the midst of the storms, it can make all the difference between joy and despair, fulfilling our purpose or living with unfulfilled dreams. Throughout this book, I've offered principles for breaking negative generational patterns. Now I'm going to focus on stories of individuals who made a positive difference and paved a way for others to continue with a positive generational legacy.

Meet Ruth. Ruth has an incredibly rich Christian heritage. Both her parents and grandparents were missionaries in Africa, and Ruth spent her childhood in Kenya. Recently, she, several of her siblings, and some extended family members were able to return to Kijabe, Kenya, to observe some of the fruits of her grandparents' planting of the Gospel. The group attended the one-hundred-year anniversary celebration of the hospital, where her dad had worked as a doctor many years before. Her dad celebrated his ninety-eighth birthday there and enjoyed returning to his birthplace. He even stood next to a "century plant" that his mother had planted when he was a baby. It was still thriving and just about as tall as he was. His vision for the hospital had been to provide training for medical professionals who would work throughout the region. Today, the hospital is training registered nurses and serves as a center for doctors in their residency training as well. Even people from other religions seek out this particular Christian hospital, as it has an excellent reputation. It was a thirty-bed hospital in 1963 when Ruth's father began working at Kijabe. Now it has grown to a 350-bed hospital!

God gave this family the privilege of witnessing His faithfulness through their father and mother's obedience to His call in Kenya. Ruth and her family were blessed to return to Africa to witness God's work through the obedience and tenacity of their mom and dad—a work that continues to thrive fifty years later. What a godly legacy imparted to this family and others! The faith of Ruth's father is powerful and lasting.

Now I'm going to tell you about a woman who lived long ago. She had to live with some very difficult circumstances. However, she had the courage not only to change her life for the better, but also to position herself so that the next generation might have a better existence.

Meet Naomi from the book of Ruth in the Old Testament. Both her husband and her sons died within a period of ten years. She was left destitute and poor. In addition, she was stuck in a foreign country. Naomi lived long ago, but if she were living in today's culture, she might be diagnosed with clinical depression. She had all of the symptoms: sadness and loss of heart for more than a two-week period, distorted thinking, and impaired judgment. I'm sure if they had any of the antidepressant medications now available, she would have taken them. She did not understand nor could she see why she was in the situation she was in. In fact, when both of her Moabite daughters-in-law tried to follow her back to her hometown, Bethlehem, in Judea, she refused. She could not see herself as being useful to anyone. Her perspective was distorted and dark, and her circumstances were not so different from the challenges that we face in our society today: working through losses, financial burdens, and job instability.

Fortunately for her, one of her daughters-in-law, Ruth, did not adopt her negative perspective and realized the positive impact that Naomi had had on her all of these years. I would imagine that when Naomi was in a good place emotionally, she gave testimony to this pagan woman about the knowledge and goodness of God and the difference He made in her life. No doubt, Ruth was not only clinging to Naomi, but wanted to cling to what she represented, which was a living God who had the power to change the course of her destiny and give hope and purpose to her life. To her credit, Naomi, even in her darkened understanding at that time, still wanted to move toward truth and not away from it. Just the idea of moving back to her homeland was a step in the right direction. She had heard in Moab that the Lord had come to the aid of His people in Judea by providing food for them, and so she decided that she would return home. This was the first good choice Naomi set in motion, which eventually turned her life around and changed both her and Ruth's destiny.

It's an application principle for our own journey as well. If we move toward God, in spite of the circumstances, even though we can't see hope at the time, God will always show up and start moving in our lives This is what happened with Ruth and Naomi. When they arrived in Bethlehem, Naomi was depressed, but still moving. Her perspective was still colored. "Don't call me Naomi," she told them. "Call me Mara, because the Almighty has made my life very bitter.

I went away full, but the Lord has brought me back empty. Why call me Naomi? The Lord has afflicted me; the Almighty has bought misfortune upon me" (Ruth 1:20, 21 NIV).

We often feel this way when we lose hope. "Hope deferred makes the heart sick, but a longing fulfilled is a tree of life" (Proverbs 13:12 NIV). The good news was that God had a plan in mind for both Ruth and Naomi and had not forgotten them. He was busy opening doors and orchestrating events on their behalf.

When we make room for God to work things out, we can have hope again. Making room means that even though we are feeling the pain of our circumstances, we can still make the right choices. Unfortunately, when circumstances get difficult, people can quickly lose both faith and heart.

If you have lived any length of time, you will know this to be true. Just when things are going well in our lives, the unexpected happens, which can cause us to doubt, question our faith, and feel hopeless. In this situation, it is difficult to find the courage not to give up.

I was busy working in my clinical practice at forty-two years old, helping people and feeling that I was making a difference in their lives, when I went in for a routine mammogram. About a week later, the results came back, and I was scheduled to see a surgeon immediately. The x-ray revealed a spot on my left breast, which required a biopsy. Within two weeks, I had a biopsy that came back malignant. I was devastated, to say the least. My son was only six years old and my daughter was in middle school. I prayed and asked God to give me direction. Any time one hears the "C" word it can be very alarming. As I was praying, Psalm 121 came up in my spirit saying, "I am watching out over your life." Those were very encouraging words from a very personal God, with whom, thankfully, I had a personal relationship. I took those encouraging words to mean that I still had a lot of life left! I believed that God was going to allow me to raise my children and still pour into the lives of others.

The treatment involved a lumpectomy the first time with twenty-one lymph nodes removed. Fortunately, the doctors did not find any cancer. I was grateful for that. I went through some chemo treatments and a full six weeks of radiation therapy. For three years, I was fine. In 1997, the cancer came back in the same breast. Even though I was grateful that the cancer was still isolated, allowing me simply to have the breast removed, the process of recovery seemed overwhelming at the time.

Part of the process involved cultivating the support of godly people who were there for me and who could encourage me when I found it difficult to encourage myself. I was fortunate in that my husband, mom, sister, and brother-in-law were very prayerful and supportive. My husband particularly helped me to fight and to be positive. His unconditional love and acceptance of me helped me to face the loss of my breast. My fear, anguish, the loss of the breast—all tested my faith on so many levels. Even though I did not always understand why this difficult situation was occurring in my life, I learned to make room for God and stand with courage and faith in a very difficult recovery process. I have been cancer free since 1997.

The Old Testament story of Ruth is another great example of a person whose faith was tested on so many levels. Ruth went through so many losses in her life, but was willing to start over with Naomi. When she left her homeland, Moab, for Bethlehem, she took a job as a humble gleaner, picking grain in the fields. Ruth did not have a victim mentality; she did not feel sorry for herself. She worked hard and did not complain about her difficult circumstances. She could have easily had the mentality of a victim, feeling sorry for herself and going around telling all of the workers in the field what she had done for Naomi and how she had lost her husband. She was just grateful for the opportunity to earn provisions for her mother-in-law and herself.

Although still in crises from leaving everything she knew behind, and experiencing losses of her own, she moved forward. God did the rest. He is always working behind the scenes on our behalf. The Bible says, "As it turned out," she found herself working in a field belonging to Boaz, who was from the clan of Elimelech. (See Ruth 2:3 NIV.)

Now here comes the restoration part of the story. Do you have your shouting voice available and your dancing shoes on? Because if God can do this for Ruth and Naomi, He can do this for you and me! Boaz was a man of resources and great integrity, who just happened to be a relative of Naomi on her late husband's side. Those relations made him a "kinsman redeemer," which meant he could be in line to continue with the family legacy by giving Ruth and Naomi economic stability. Now if Naomi, the bitter and depressed mother-in-law who was going through such losses, decided to stay where she was in Moab, and not move toward God in some way, they would never have been in the position to meet Boaz. (Being obedient to take positive steps is really important when it comes to changing your circumstances!) Now where Naomi could see no hope, there is hope again. When she had no hope, there was no vision or possibility. Now she has both. Naomi suddenly wakes up from the darkness she had been in and remembers who he is. "The Lord bless him!" Naomi said to her daughter-in-law. "He has not stopped showing his kindness to the living and the dead." She added, "That man is our close relative; he is one of our guardian-redeemers" (Ruth 2:20 NIV). Naomi is now beginning to realize that Boaz's interest in Ruth can lead to a restored life! Naomi encourages the young Ruth to communicate her interest in Boaz as well. As a result, Ruth and Boaz fall in love and he asks for her hand in marriage. This is where the beautiful love story begins. Although Boaz was in line to redeem Naomi and Ruth's financial situation, there was a closer relative, who was in line before him, and was due to inherit the estate of Ruth's husband. However, in order to secure the man's inheritance he also had to take the widow Ruth. Since the closer relative did not want to do that, Boaz moved quickly to accomplish this goal. He did so with integrity, honesty, and forthrightness.

Of course, the story ends with Ruth and Boaz getting married and carrying on the family legacy. Where the lineage had stopped with the death of Naomi's sons (see Figure 4.1), now the possibility of new life and new generations existed. Where the legacy before was destroyed by death and poverty, now we have life and resources flowing again. God always has a plan, and when we open up to Him and are obedient to His voice, He has an abundant life waiting for us.

The chart in Figure 4.2 shows how the choices of Ruth and Naomi reversed the destruction that was present in their family system. They both moved toward God in spite of their very difficult circumstances. Naomi moved toward Bethlehem where she wanted to be with safe friends and God's people again. She left Moab and Ruth followed her. Ruth communicated her devotion and love for her bitter and old mother-in-law who, at the time, had nothing to offer her. Yet, it must have been Naomi's faith in the living God that had sealed her commitment to follow her. We hear nothing about the other daughter-in-law, whose name was Orpah. She descended into anonymity after she decided to stay in Moab.

The positive generational legacy began many years prior because of a choice that a former prostitute and pagan woman made when she heard about the mighty wonders of God and how He helped His people move to a new land. Her name was Rahab and she lived in Jericho. She hid the Hebrew spies when they came to check out the land that God promised to give them. When the walls came tumbling down, God protected her and her family and she eventually married one of the Israelite spies. She was then adopted into God's family. (See Figure 5.) She had the courage early on, like Ruth, to follow the God of Abraham, Isaac, and Jacob, even though everything in her culture and beliefs were against it. If you look at the chart in Figure 5, you will see how the negative generational cycle was reversed with

Rahab. She married a Hebrew and became the ancestor of Boaz, the kinsman redeemer through Naomi's late husband, who married Ruth, and their grandson was Obed, who became Naomi's grandson also through Boaz! Obed was an important person—the grandfather of David, who eventually became King over Israel. If you continue reading the generational legacy, you will see that Jesus comes out of this lineage. How amazing is it that God chose a willing prostitute, Rahab, and a pagan Moabite woman, Ruth, to be adopted into His family!

How exciting to know that it does not matter where you come from, though it does matter where you are headed. If you have been adopted into the family of the kingdom of God, then you are headed for a life filled with peace, joy, and wonderful and exciting adventures!

Figure 4: Generational Legacy: Choices that Lead to Death or Life

1. Death

2. Life

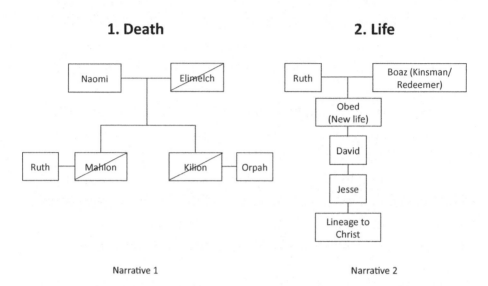

Narrative 1

Narrative 2

Figure 5: Generational Legacy of Rahab and Ruth Adopted into the Legacy of Jesus Christ

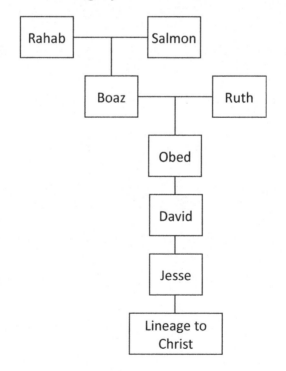

CHAPTER 9

Forgiving Others, Forgiving Ourselves

Be agreeable, be sympathetic, be loving, be compassionate, be humble. That goes for all of you, no exceptions. No retaliation. No sharp-tongued sarcasm. Instead, bless—that's your job, to bless. You'll be a blessing and also get a blessing.

—1 PETER 3:8-9 (MSG)

Throughout this book, we have talked about how negative generational patterns can repeat if we are not aware of these patterns and how to change them. As believers, finding out who we are in Christ is essential to breaking these patterns. In addition, there is another important concept that I need to emphasize, because it is a key principle in breaking generational patterns. That is the concept of forgiving others and ourselves.

Forgiveness is the intentional act of letting go of feelings of resentment and anger toward a person or persons who have offended you. The process of forgiveness is a difficult one to work through, as there are times when people really suffer tremendous violations at the hands of others. Examples are: people who have been sexually abused, a mother who preferred connections to substances like drugs instead of being present with her children, a person who has been physically abused or abandoned, a spouse that has violated the marriage with affairs, or, as you will read about later in the chapter, a person whose own mother tried to murder him.

The heart of a person who has been violated can be wounded and scarred so severely that it does not want to forgive. Although some circumstances may appear justified, harboring negative emotions related to unforgiveness has a devastating effect on the person who is holding onto the resentments. People who hang on to unforgiveness often go through life bitter and resentful, and may have a difficult time seeing people in a positive light and/or trusting others. As a result, they can lean toward isolation and never experience the deep, connected relationships they were created for. Unforgiveness hinders us from living our best lives! Unforgiveness toward others can also lead to lost and fractured relationships. Unforgiveness of ourselves can cause us to self-sabotage and hinder us from accomplishing our God-given purpose. An illustration of this principle can be observed in a person who has experienced some failures, becoming so self-critical that he/ she gives up and does not pursue his or her dreams anymore.

On the other hand, a great example in Scripture of an individual who guarded his heart from unforgiveness is Joseph, the son of Jacob. His dad considered him the favored son, and his brothers were very angry about this. Therefore, as soon as an opportunity came, they sold him into slavery and told their father that an animal had killed their brother. Even though Joseph went through some very difficult times, he purposed to trust God and move forward. He not only had the difficult task of learning a new culture (because he was sold into slavery in Egypt), but he was also falsely accused of sexually violating his boss's wife. Although this was untrue, he was thrown into prison for his alleged betrayal.

Joseph could have become really bitter, and no one would have blamed him for that. Instead, he continued to persevere and do the job that was in front of him. Everywhere he went he practiced faith and integrity and kept a positive focus. God had a great plan for him, and when the time came for God to promote him, he went from prisoner to governor overnight! I'm sure the timing took a lot longer than Joseph expected, but he remained positive and faithful while he was in prison. Promotion was coming. Two of the Pharaoh's employees, the chief cupbearer and the chief baker, were thrown into prison with him because they had angered Pharaoh. Joseph volunteered to interpret their dreams.

He was zealous and instantly ready to help with the dream interpretation. He could have said, Sorry, I can't help you. After all, I don't know why God put me in this dungeon. Do not ask me, I have enough problems! Instead, when he saw that they were dejected, he asked them "Why do you look so sad today?" (Genesis 40:7 NIV). They told him that they had dreams, but there was no one to interpret them. Now right there, Joseph could have felt sorry for himself and told them that his brothers and God had both forsaken him. And that interpreting dreams only got him in trouble. He could have wallowed in self-pity, but he didn't. He immediately told them that the interpretation of dreams belonged to God and that he was able to give them insight into their dreams. As a result, just as Joseph told them, the chief cupbearer was restored to his position and the other man was executed by hanging.

At this point in his experience, Joseph could have gotten very bitter and resentful again, as he had asked the cupbearer to remember him. He said, "'But when all goes well with you, remember me and show me kindness, mention me to Pharaoh and get me out of this prison. I was forcibly carried off from the land of the Hebrews, and even here I have done nothing to deserve being put in a dungeon' .... The chief cupbearer did not remember Joseph; he forgot him" (Genesis 40:14-15, 23 NIV).

Two full years passed and then Pharaoh had a dream. This is when the cupbearer finally remembered Joseph and his ability to interpret dreams. Pharaoh called for Joseph immediately. Joseph interpreted a dream that Pharaoh had about seven fat cows and seven skinny cows. The dreams represented that there would be a season of plenty and then there would be a season of famine. Joseph also gave Pharaoh a plan for how to manage the food resources when there was a good harvest so that when the famine came, they would be prepared. Since Joseph had such wisdom, and God's Spirit clearly was with him and in him, Pharaoh selected Joseph to be the governing ruler over the entire land of Egypt.

After seven years of a good economy, the season started to change and the famine came, just as Joseph had interpreted. When the famine hit Canaan, his brothers had to travel to Egypt to ask for food. Little did they know that they would eventually meet up with their brother again, who was now fully in charge.

Here was Joseph's opportunity for revenge. He could have said, well, now I'm in charge and I've been through a lot because of you, so I'm going to make you all suffer! I'm going to withhold the food you need so you can suffer just like I did. However, after a time of initial testing to see if his brothers had remorse about what they did, he eventually revealed himself and made a way to provide for his family and extended family, including all of the tribes. They were all invited to move to Egypt where Joseph made sure that there were adequate provisions for them and a section of land to occupy. He could now see the purpose for all of his suffering; he could now see the bigger picture.

> Joseph said to his brothers, "I am Joseph your brother whom you sold into Egypt. But don't feel badly, don't blame yourselves for selling me. God was behind it. God sent me here ahead of you to save lives. There

has been a famine in the land now for two years; the famine will continue for five more years—neither plowing nor harvesting. God sent me on ahead to pave the way and make sure there was a remnant in the land, to save your lives in an amazing act of deliverance. So you see, it wasn't you who sent me here but God. He set me in place as a father to Pharaoh, put me in charge of his personal affairs, and made me ruler of all Egypt. (Genesis 45:4-8 MSG)

Joseph was able to reframe his thinking about the situation. As a result, he and his brothers, and his father, were able to live out the end of their days together. This is a beautiful story of forgiveness, hope, redemption, and reconciliation.

In my own personal experience helping others to work through forgiveness, I have come to one conclusion: that we need God's help to forgive others. We all have the ability to choose to forgive by an act of our will. However, the feelings of forgiveness don't always follow. We all have "triggers"–something that happens that reminds us of the offense. Then our minds go into overdrive, reminding and recreating the offense, replaying it over and over, causing us to go back toward unforgiveness.

Applying God's love to the offense helps us to begin to think differently. By incorporating His love with our choice to forgive, suddenly something amazing happens. Our minds are now focused on God's love toward us and how much He has forgiven us for our offenses and sins. All of a sudden our perspective changes. Instead of focusing on the offense, we are looking back and remembering all of the times God forgave us and granted forgiveness for our misdeeds or shortcomings.

In addition, as we focus on our relationship with Him, and realize that He is able to restore what has been lost, broken, and damaged, then we can let unforgiveness go and begin to incorporate a new focus into our lives. The new focus is on trusting God to do new and great things in us since His plan for us is good and not evil, to give us a hope and a future. (See Jeremiah 29:11.)

I know of no more poignant and dramatic illustration of this principle than the testimony of Rick Leavenworth. I had an opportunity to meet Rick and his lovely wife, Esther, a couple of years ago. It was easy to look past his disability because of his welcoming smile and active, engaging passion for life. He is like a modern-day Joseph in many ways, and definitely a man of whom anyone would say: he has a right to be bitter, angry, and resentful; he has a right to refuse to forgive. On a hot summer day in 1961, four-year-old Ricky Leavenworth innocently jogged across the desert sand to play with his mom. That would be the last time his legs took him anywhere. Here is his story, in his own words:

> I was beside myself with excitement as Mom loaded my older sister, Kathy, and me into our old Buick for a road trip heading east on Highway 66 to Arizona. Just outside of Barstow, California, as we rolled through the sweltering Mohave Desert, the car groaned, sputtered, and then slowed to a stop as Mom steered onto the shoulder. "We're out of gas," she said.

> Mom sat for a long while in silence, staring out into the desert. Three cars had driven by, but they did not stop. Mom sighed heavily and uttered, "I guess no one cares." She opened her door and walked to the back of the car, opened the trunk and took some things out. Then came to the passenger side where I sat. Mom was holding a yellow quilt as she opened the door and said, "Let's go play a game, Ricky." We

walked away from the car and disappeared over a nearby dirt mound as Kathy watched from the back seat of the Buick.

As Mom and I crested the mound, a boy's wonderland came into view—a small junk dump site. As I started off to investigate, Mom stopped me. "Calm down, Ricky, come here. We're going to play Blind Man's Bluff."

Mom motioned me over to where she was standing on the yellow quilt she had laid out on the sandy desert. She tied a white handkerchief over my eyes so I couldn't see her, but little did she know that in the bright afternoon sun, I could see Mom's outline easily through the thin material. I stood there innocently watching as Mom backed up several steps. She appeared to be frustrated with something in her hands that she was fiddling with. I then heard a metallic click-clack and saw two bright flashes of blinding light as a deafening POP-POP echoed across the barren desert.

Everything then moved in slow motion as excruciating pain and fear assaulted my little body. I suddenly felt numb. I collapsed to my knees and then fell face first onto the yellow quilt. I remember struggling to get up, but I couldn't move anything except my arms. I rose up on my elbows crying in painful fear for mom's help. Mom grabbed the blindfold off my eyes and disappeared over the dirt mound. She was headed to the car where Kathy was. In my confusion, I saw that the yellow quilt was turning crimson red, but I didn't understand why.

Later I did understand. My mother had shot me in the chest.

As I watched through fearful, tear-clouded eyes, I saw mom reappear over the dirt mound dragging Kathy by her arm. Kathy then saw me.

My eight-year-old sister saved my life that day. Somehow, her pleas to get help for me snapped Mom's altered mind back into reality. Suddenly, Mom looked back at me, and then back at Kathy, and then looked at the pistol in her hand. Gasping, she dropped the gun. "My God, what have I done?" she said. Then she literally ran out onto the highway waving her arms and the white handkerchief hysterically in an attempt to stop a passer-by. Eventually, a highway transportation worker stopped his service truck and called the local dispatcher on his radio, who in turn notified the highway patrol and ambulance service.

That Good Samaritan will surely never forget that day, and I'm forever grateful to him for stopping. Imagine his shock to find a small, sunburned boy lying in a pool of blood. I did not find out until many years later that if my heart had not been slightly rotated in my chest cavity from a birth defect, the bullet would have pierced it, and I would have died almost instantly.

Following my mother's arrest, she was diagnosed with paranoid schizrenia, and then committed to a mental institution. Although my mother received treatment over the years, the voices never seemed to cease, and she periodically checked herself into a hospital for care during the remaining years of her life.

In retrospect, God's hand quickly intervened that day. His timing was perfect, and soon I was in the hospital having blood transfusions and emergency surgery. Later that night, when I was in surgical recovery, I heard through all of the recovery room sounds what I thought was a familiar voice on the other side of the pulled curtain. Was that my daddy? I thought to myself, "Everything is going to be okay, now that my daddy's here." I was so relieved to hear his voice, but something was different; there was a seriousness about it that I hadn't heard before as he talked to the doctor.

"When will he be able to walk again and come home?" I heard a long pause of silence as the doctor hesitated to answer. "No, I'm afraid you don't understand … he will never be able to walk again." The hectic sounds of the recovery room faded away as my hearing focused in on my daddy's voice. Then I drifted back into a fearful sleep due to what I had just heard and the effects of the anesthesia. That was the only time I ever heard my daddy weeping.

I spent nine long, lonely years in hospitals and in physical rehabilitation centers. During that time, I had to have daily physical therapy to help me regain my strength. In addition, I endured eleven surgeries to continually correct my hips and legs as they grew. The hardest part of those long years were the nights when I would cry myself to sleep with overwhelming feelings of loneliness, being unwanted, unloved, untouched, full of fear, and insecurity.

It was a bittersweet transition to finally go home, at age thirteen, and return to a daily family and school schedule. Home life was great, but I was often teased and bullied at school because of my disability and lack of proper education. Even harder to work through was my anger toward God, whom I didn't really know, and at my mother—even though dad had explained that she was sick—and toward myself, believing myself unworthy and undeserving of love, friendships, or a normal life. Those years were very tough and painful. I threw my leg braces against the wall more times than I can remember, not being able to reconcile my disabled condition with my mother's rejection of me, while trying to comprehend what I might have done to deserve such a fate. I turned my anger inward—poisoning myself with bitterness at life and the bad hand I had been dealt.

In my teen years, I chose to leave my "special needs" high school to be mainstreamed into regular public high school in order to receive better academics and education levels. It was during these strenuous years that I contemplated suicide several times, as I could not see where I could possibly fit into society or be of any use or endearment to anyone.

Then God revealed His love for me in the summer of 1976. At age nineteen, I accepted Christ as my Savior and my lifelong question "Why me?" was answered by 2 Corinthians 12:9-10 that talks about letting

God help me to be strong in my weakness, even in my disability. As a young Christian in the faith, I learned of God's unending forgiveness and care that had watched over me, when I was shot and through multiple surgeries and hospitals as I grew. He plucked me out of a very bad situation in 1961 and placed me in a safer environment where He could protect me and save me from further harm or evil doings. God saved me for something much better. Jesus paid the price with His own life in order that I would be freed from my own darkness, my own slavish sin.

However, I had to come to terms with my disability and how I was going to live. Was I to become bitter or better? I had to separate the physical limitations that I had from the world's mindset that I was a weak invalid. I had to change that channel and learn how valued I was in God's eyes, and that I was bought with the high price of Jesus' life on the cross so that I could have a full and meaningful life. I learned that my real disability had not been paralyzed legs, but rather a paralyzed heart in not knowing Jesus Christ.

I also learned about Joseph in the Bible and realized my story had many similarities. I read how Joseph forgave his brothers' evil deeds and how God made good out of those evil circumstances. I understood then that in order for me to be healed more and to move forward, I had to forgive my mother. But that wasn't easy for me. Our family rarely discussed deep, emotional things. We had rarely even discussed what happened the day my mother shot me. I didn't know where to start or how to go about this idea of true, honest forgiveness.

Then I met Esther in the summer of 1977, a year after I had accepted Christ as my Lord and Savior. God used Esther in multiple ways to break down the walls of self-protection I had erected in my heart many years earlier. Those barriers kept people, especially women, at arm's length so I wouldn't be deeply injured again. Nevertheless, because of this one lady's attention, attraction, and genuine caring for me, the barriers began to crumble. God used Esther to help me on this path of forgiveness.

On another hot sweltering day in 1978, Esther and I went to see my mom in the Apple Valley area where she lived in a small mobile home in a roadside trailer park. God had helped soften my heart toward my mom during the previous year, and Esther gave me the encouragement I needed. Finally, I could go to my mom and say those life-changing, wound-healing words: "Mom, I forgive you for what you did that day. Even though I don't have the use of my legs, Jesus has healed me on the inside, and I am okay with what happened. I don't blame you, mom, I blame Satan because he meant it for evil purposes, he meant to destroy our family, he meant to kill me. But God in His mighty power, grace, and love has made good out of those circumstances. I love you, Mom."

Mom's tears flowed down her cheeks as she heard those long-awaited healing words of forgiveness. I could only forgive my mom because I myself had been totally forgiven and renewed by Christ. Discussing my forgiveness of her naturally flowed into the discussion of God's forgiveness of her too, as I desperately wanted my mom to know the same cleansing relief I had experienced by developing a lifelong relationship with Jesus Christ. I had been forgiven, and I wanted her to know the forgiveness of Christ also. So it naturally led to my sharing God's plan of salvation with her. That day began her eternity-long relationship with Jesus Christ. I went to mom that day with the purpose of helping her wounds to heal and went away with my own wounds healed as well.

One of the last wonderful memories I have before my mom left this life and entered into heaven's rest was when she would walk up to new arrivals at the assisted living home where she stayed, look them in the eyes and ask with a glowing smile on her face, "Do you know Jesus?"

That, my friends, is the power of God's forgiveness, with Christ's awesome power and love being administered through one who was willing to rise above his circumstances. It's God's inside out, upside down way of doing things, using me, "the victim," to forgive first, and then point my mom to God's forgiveness and salvation.

What is amazing about Rick Leavenworth is that he did not allow his disability to get in the way of his ability to have purpose and to significantly contribute to society. He has worked hard all of his life and has had diverse careers paths leading to his current position, which he has held over thirty-two years. He worked his way up from an engineering draftsman to a Computer Animated Graphics Specialist for a major aerospace corporation.

Working through the process of unforgiveness is not easy. It takes work and the processing of negative emotions. It can be difficult to look at the situation and the person, inasmuch as doing so might trigger memories that remind us of losses or past painful times we want to forget. Rick admits that he is still a product of what he has experienced in life, both the good and the bad. His painful youth and lack of any self-esteem creeps back in from time to time, and takes him down for a round or two, sometimes three or four rounds. But God is faithful.

Getting unstuck is no easy task, but it does help if we can obtain insight into what the offending person experienced or suffered in his or her past. More often than not, the person who hurt you has been hurt by someone before you came along. It is helpful to realize that there was something broken inside of him or her, and that pain was carried into the next close relationship or to the next generation. Rick's mom was mentally ill. Perhaps your parent was abused by a parent or close relative, and their automatic response is to abuse in a similar way. Perhaps a spouse was abandoned and rejected when young, and now when life gets challenging, he or she responds by rejecting you. When you can understand the difficulty that the offending person has gone through, it is easier to have compassion for the offender.

This in no way excuses the behavior. However, it does help the process of learning to forgive so that we don't repeat the offending person's pattern and become destructive to ourselves or others. When we see the destructiveness of unforgiveness, such as in fragmented and bitter families, unhealthy relationships, depression, and hopelessness, we often will run toward the idea of choosing to forgive, so that the next generation has a good inheritance, one that provides a platform for propagating positive generational fruit. Where there was hopelessness before, now there is peace; where sadness, now joy; where shattered relationships, now authentic, healthy relationships. It was true for Joseph, it is true for Rick Leavenworth, and it can be true for you. Rick's story of horror, survival, struggle, determination, forgiveness, faith, and courage inspired Hollywood film director, Lee Stanley, to produce the documentary "Mountain Tops," and then take both the film and Rick to some of America's toughest, at-risk youth, changing their lives with his testimony. If his story can change lives, what will yours do? Our God is the God of the impossible!

Below are some principles to help you to learn how to forgive:

1. Invite God's love into your life to help you forgive. Ask Him to help you see forgiveness through His eyes, not your own.

2. Be willing to process and talk about negative feelings related to an offense with someone safe. You don't need to feel guilty about having negative feelings, as they are part of being human and working through an offense. The key is not staying parked in the unforgiveness camp.

3. As you are working through an offense, take the opportunity to learn more about yourself and how you generally handle offenses that come your way. Is there a pattern of how you handle an offense? Do you shut people out, withdraw, and cut people off without desiring reconciliation?

4. Sometimes a current offense can pull up past offenses and cause us to misdirect anger or overreact. It is sometimes helpful to journal so that there is more understanding about what may be going on emotionally so that you don't overreact.

5. Practice being a fast forgiver. Learn to let go of offenses quickly so that they don't stay with you and build up resentments. This has to have an intentional focus of not allowing offenses to attach to you emotionally, like barnacles attaching to a ship

6. Remember that forgiveness is for you, not for anyone else. However, forgiveness does not always include reconciliation. Of course, we would always want to have a heart toward reconciliation, but that takes two people who both desire reconciliation, and sometimes requires significant changes that people are not willing to make. For example, I may forgive the person who has abused me in the past, but I am not willing to allow abuse again, so the relationship may not be able to be reconciled.

Life is often not fair; but God is still faithful. If we continue to focus on the unfairness that life brings, we will always be disappointed. You don't have to look far to see injustices in our society. However, God is merciful, just, and faithful, and He will make up for the lack that you may be experiencing in your life. He has all of the necessary resources, and He desires to love and bless the life that is submitted to Him!

ABOUT THE AUTHOR

DR. MARY SIMMS has over twenty-five years of professional counseling and speaking experience, working with families and individuals in the areas of marriage and family, relationships, abuse, addiction, and recovery. Dr. Simms has worked and taught at the university level as well as in hospital and corporate settings, and is currently in private practice. Throughout her career, she has been recognized as a voice of hope, helping thousands live better quality lives. Having grown up in the inner city and experiencing firsthand the effects of violence and abuse, she understands the journey of moving past pain to achieve a God-given purpose. Dr. Simms is also a two-time cancer survivor, familiar with the amazing power of God to heal, redeem, and restore.

Dr. Simms was a contributor to Susan Osborn's books *Wounded by Words, Too Soon to Say Goodbye,* and *Invisible Chains.* She has also published articles entitled "Starting Over," and "Deep Valleys" in *Just Women's Magazine.* She has traveled internationally with LifeBranch Institute International, a nonprofit marriage and family ministry designed to strengthen families and relationships.

Contact Dr. Simms at: www.familyoutreachcounseling.com
She would love to hear from you.